THE CATCH

THE CATCH

Families, Fishing, and Faith

William J. Vande Kopple

William B. Eerdmans Publishing Company
Grand Rapids, Michigan / Cambridge, U.K.

Wm. B. Eerdmans Publishing Co.

255 Jefferson Ave. S.E., Grand Rapids, Michigan 49503 /
P.O. Box 163, Cambridge CB3 9PU U.K.

Printed in the United States of America

08 07 06 05 04   7 6 5 4 3 2 1

ISBN 0-8028-2677-6

www.eerdmans.com

Contents

Preface   vii

Acknowledgments   xi

Sex Ed: My Early Years   1

The Wall   11

Bottom Feeders   16

Clear and Pure   22

In the Dark   31

Too Good to Be True?   39

The Path of the Wind   45

The Soul's Sincere Desire?   66

Frogs   71

Wilderness Survival Kit   75

Through All Generations   89

Separation Syndrome   99

All Sufficient?   109

Brothers Forever   114

A New Earth   141

Heart Trouble   147

For the Morrow   158

Through the Ice   177

Still Fishing   188

Yesterday, Today, and Tomorrow   207

Preface

These days, those with even moderate interest in the nature of written texts spend a significant amount of time debating the issue of genre. As these debaters lay out their positions, they almost always present their views of the relationship between the world projected in a text and the world in which I, for example, waded stretches of the Manistee River three days before writing this sentence and caught three honey-colored king salmon. Unfortunately, these people often use such a large number of seemingly self-contradictory phrases (such as *nonfiction narrative* and *narrative reportage*) that their presentations can be difficult to follow.

So I will try to be as clear and concise as possible: The pieces collected here are fiction inspired by but only loosely related to fact.

In these pieces, I do refer to a large number of actual places in Iowa and Michigan, places that you might be able to find if you wanted to. For instance, you might well be able to locate the Snows-Channel resort that I use as a setting in such pieces as "Through All Generations" and "Still Fishing." But you would almost certainly have to be on the water of the channel to spot it and its prominent dock, not on any road. You could drive to the

Sylvania Tract and set out to discover East Bear Lake, which I describe in "A New Earth." But to find it you would have to paddle across two sizable lakes and then negotiate a long and uneven portage trail. You could even hike out the peninsula in Wilderness State Park that ends in Waugoshance Point, looking to the south in hopes of spotting those two enormous fish-attracting boulders I describe in "Wilderness Survival Kit." But the hike is so long and the number of boulders so large that your chances of success are, practically speaking, nonexistent.

In these pieces, I also use the actual names of some of my relatives. But not all of the names in these stories correspond to real people. After reading "The Path of the Wind," one of my sons wondered whether I have an uncle and aunt that he somehow had never been able to meet. I do not. When I do use actual relatives' names, I do so, I think, because these names and all that I associate with them serve for me as reliable emotional touchstones and as productive invention aids.

Finally, some of the actions that I present in these pieces resemble what actually happened at various times in my family's life. But not everything presented here actually happened, and if some actions presented here did in fact once occur, they did not necessarily happen in the order and within the context in which I present them. Once I developed these pieces to the point that they picked up some momentum, I had the surprising and intriguing sensation of watching them begin to assume their own trajectory. But in all that I did with them, I never stopped seeking the truth.

Many people made it possible and enjoyable for me to remember, notice, reflect, craft, polish, and dare to publish.

I owe a great debt to Wanda, Jon, Joel, and Jason as well as to my extended family. From them came the core of my emotional support. From them came most of the questions or little rubs from which stories grew. From them came reminders about and refinements of memories. And from them came much of my knowledge of and appreciation for stories. Around campfires at state parks, in the dorm lounge up at the station, in pontoon boats and fishing boats and canoes, and on hikes along beaches, we have told one another some great stories.

I also am thankful to many friends and many of my colleagues at Calvin College for encouraging me to think that working on what they called my "fishing stories" was not an utter waste of time. Some of these folks went well beyond such encouragement. They gave me helpful specific responses to stories or parts of stories, they invited me to read to supportive groups, and they even suggested or found outlets for some of these pieces. Among these folks are the following: Marlys Admiraal, Roy Anker, the late Lionel Basney, Ed Ericson, Susan Felch, George Harper, Denice O'Heron, the late Carol Post, John H. Timmerman, Elizabeth Vander Lei, Clare Walhout, and Dean Ward.

My colleagues Gary Schmidt and Jim Vanden Bosch belong in a special category. These two sometimes joke about pairing up to form a team of literary agents. They would, I imagine, differ markedly from each other in their styles of working with authors and publishers. But they would be effective, perhaps even formidably effective. They certainly did agent-like work for me, on more than one occasion. I hope that none of the pieces gathered here is an embarrassment to either of them.

Finally, I wish to express my appreciation to several people at Eerdmans Publishing Company. I thank William B. Eerdmans, Jr., for his early and steady support of this project. I thank Willem Mineur for giving me choices, interesting choices, about how the book would look. And I thank my editor, Jenny Hoffman, for the persistent yet gentle way she worked to shape this book, helping to turn what I sent her into something a bit different from what I had expected but something better than I had foreseen.

Acknowledgments

S everal of the pieces included in this collection originally appeared in other publications. And some of them appeared in a form slightly different from the form in which they appear here. It is a pleasure to express my gratitude to the following parties for permission to reprint the listed pieces:

- Thanks to the editors of the Calvin College *Dialogue* for permission to reprint "The Wall," "Yesterday, Today, and Tomorrow," "A New Earth," and "Heart Trouble."
- Thanks to the editors of *Perspectives* for permission to reprint "Bottom Feeders," "Clear and Pure," "Trolling Time" (now titled "Through All Generations"), "Separation Syndrome," "Too Good to Be True?" "All Sufficient?" and "The Soul's Sincere Desire?"
- Thanks to the editors of *The American Enterprise,* a national magazine of politics, business, and culture (TAEmag.com), for permission to reprint "Frogs" and "Fishing around in the Dark" (now titled "In the Dark").
- Thanks to the editors and publishers of *Winter: A Spiritual Biography of the Season,* by Gary Schmidt and Susan M. Felch (Woodstock, VT: SkyLight Paths Publishing, 2003), for permission to reprint "Through the Ice."

Sex Ed: My Early Years

As I look back to my boyhood, I realize that I blundered on my own through whole territories of notions about sex and should really have had a constant, expert, and gentle guide.

When I was really young, I remember, I didn't even have a clear idea about which of my body parts were supposed to be special in some way. One humid July Saturday, my dad and mom took my two younger brothers and me wading and paddling in a crystalline little creek near the Silver Lake sand dunes. Afterwards, since we three boys whined about the prospect of riding home in wet suits and getting itchy bun disease, and since there were no bathhouses or restrooms anywhere along the creek, my mom decided that we boys should do a quick change outside the car in the gravel parking lot.

"Just stand on your flip-flops, pull off your suit, and stay close to the car," she said, "and I'll come down the line to dry you off. Then you can hustle up and pull on your underpants." So I tugged that clinging suit off — first one side down an inch, then the other, until finally it fell — and I stood facing a couple of other families across from us in the parking lot.

"Billy! Turn around right now," my mom hissed. "In front

those are your private parts. It's not so bad if other people see your fanny."

But I put a little resistance in my shoulders as she tried to spin me. I didn't have any clear idea of what a private part was, but somehow I had developed the notion that I should try as hard as I could to keep others from seeing my skinny white butt. Eventually I had to let her turn me around and dry me off, but I was embarrassed that those people across the parking lot were then able to size up my buns, and I spent most of the ride home wondering about what was so bad about my front.

When I was older, about seven or eight, my mom found me engrossed in one of the Tarzan movies often shown in those days right after kids got home from school. Tarzan had just wrestled himself out of the coils of a river python, and he had limped to a bubbling hot spring surrounded by exotic-looking ferns. There he would soothe, I assumed, his bruised muscles. A moment after he eased into the pool, I heard a rustle and Jane approached through the shoulder-high ferns. She walked to the edge of the pool, gave Tarzan a very faint smile, and then slowly raised her arms to the back of her neck to start untying the knot that held her skimpy jungle suit up.

Now this was a movie made in the fifties, so as she worked the knot loose, the camera switched from Jane to the spot on the ground where her suit fell in a small heap. Then it moved to Tarzan's face. I watched the light in his eyes as I could hear Jane stepping into the water. By the time the camera got back to Jane, she was drifting over to Tarzan's side of the pool. The surface of the water was bubbly and wavy, and it was hard to see below the surface, but it sure seemed to me that she wasn't wearing any underwear and that her buns were much fuller than mine.

It was when she started to bring her feet under her and extend her arms to Tarzan that my mom walked in and figured out what I was watching. Looking back, I realize that she didn't overreact. "Billy," she said as she turned off the television, "maybe you shouldn't be watching all these jungle movies when you have a perfectly good backyard to play in. Why don't you spend more time outside? But remember: If you ever have any questions about the male body or the female body or sexual relations, you should feel free to talk to Dad. You will go to him if you have questions, won't you?"

"Sure," I said. But I had no idea what sexual relations were, and I was pretty sure I had never heard people sitting around talking about them. I decided I should find out more about what sexual relations were before I started asking my dad questions about them, questions that would probably turn out to be stupid and embarrassing.

Most of the neighborhood boys were about my age or younger, and they admitted that they had never heard the words "sexual" and "relations" right next to each other like that. The one older boy on our street, Eugene, who kept a German shepherd that had been trained as an attack dog and had forgotten none of his training, sized me up for quite a while after I asked him about sexual relations and then just muttered that "you'd better wait a year or so until your special assembly at school."

During the next school year I waited eagerly for a special assembly, and there was one, but I wasn't invited. The teachers said that all the girls were to proceed to the basement auditorium for a meeting that would last an hour, and while they were gone we boys left behind would have a study hall, even though we practically had to make up stuff to work on. When the girls came back, they were in little packs of giggles and whispers, and they all were unusually smug, wearing looks that said "we know something important that you don't know and you're going to have to be really nice to us to get us to tell you about it." Occasionally, one of them would use a word like "prepubescent" as she glanced over at us boys, a word that none of us knew, but we were all too lazy to look it up and either too proud or too afraid to ask them for an explanation.

Almost exactly a year later, all of us boys finally got our turn to be summoned to the school basement. The principal told us that we were going to learn some very important things, and if we messed around, the assembly would be cancelled and a letter would be sent home to our parents. Then Dr. Utenbrood, the dad of the smartest but laziest kid in our class, turned down the lights and put up an overhead transparency. On it were words that sounded a lot alike but that looked foreign to me: maturation, menstruation, ovulation, copulation, ejaculation, fertilization, and gestation. As he picked at his nose a little bit, he mumbled a quick sentence or two about each of these terms. It was too dark for us to take any notes.

Then he showed a short film about what looked like tadpoles working frantically to move ahead in a gently curving narrow stream. They were working so hard that I felt sorry for them. Usually only one of them, Dr. Utenbrood said, ever really reached his goal.

Finally, he showed black-and-white drawings of what he called the "male and female reproductive systems." I spent most of my time focusing on the female system, but it looked like something for a Rorschach test, with small circles, looping tubes, and a bigger cylinder. The doctor pointed to parts of the sketch and gave us names to remember, but I would have needed a handout to keep all of those new words straight. At the end of his talk, the doctor asked if any of us had any questions, any questions at all. We looked to the left and the right and behind us, but no one said a word.

I left with the vague notion that for me to have a baby someday, a sperm cell from me had to search around and find an egg in a girl's body and then fight to get into the egg. But I wasn't sure how the sperm managed to get into the girl's body or what part of her body that sperm would have to be on the lookout for.

On the way back to class, I had to stop in the bathroom. It was there that I had one of the two or three most intense educational experiences of my life. In the corner, Brent, the kid in our class who had more zits than anyone else, was standing facing a semicircle of eager-looking guys. When I came in, he waved me over, and, without really thinking about it, I joined the group. He claimed to have found a stash of dirty magazines in his dad's closet, and he was now expanding on Dr. Utenbrood's talk. But he was using words Dr. Utenbrood had never used, words like *beaver* and *boner* and *boink*.

As I listened, it finally hit me that if I were ever to have children, I would probably have to be naked or close to naked and somehow put what I now knew as my main private part into a naked woman's main private part and that in some way little sperm cells from me would have to be persuaded to swim over to her private part and then head up a channel inside her on their own.

I grew so lightheaded that I stumbled out of the bathroom and crouched down between a radiator and a wall while I tried to slow my breathing. I was right at the stage in my life when I was afraid of having anyone, including members of my own family, see me undressed. I always locked the bathroom door when I took a shower and never even walked around the house in my underwear. And though I more and more often had worked up the nerve to walk home from school with Joanie, who lived a couple of streets over from me and often seemed to be waiting for me after school, and though I had begun to think about asking her if she wanted to hold hands once in a while, the thought of seeing her even in her underwear was one my mind couldn't hold on to for more than a couple of seconds. The thought of being naked with her was somewhere between disgusting and horrifying.

How in the world was a person supposed to get prepared to do something like that? All that touching and seeing private parts and working to fit together. It was all way too open. Besides, what would happen if you were so close and had to clear your throat, or worse, cough or sneeze or burp?

I began to develop a somewhat twisted view of sex and reproduction. And unfortunately, I wasn't getting any help in straightening this view out. I had always been too embarrassed to ask my dad any questions about sex. Plus after the episode in the boys' bathroom it didn't take me too long to figure out that somehow my dad and mom must have tried some sex out — at least once — in order for me to be born, and that was an idea I tried really hard to deny. "They just couldn't have done that, not my own mom and dad — maybe I came from somewhere else," I would repeat to myself.

Nothing in my church helped me very much either. We never talked in Sunday school or catechism about sexual relations. And we never heard sermons about whether sex was a blessing or a curse.

One time, though, a guest pastor used a few verses from the Song of Solomon as his text for a sermon about how much pure delight Christ takes in his church. But once I had opened to the verses that the minister read, I started to look through the rest of the book. I almost started to feel faint again. "Your stature is like that of the palm," I read, "and your breasts like clusters of fruit."

"Who would ever talk like that?" I wondered. "Who could think up such things? Does God have thoughts about human sex? How in the world did these words get into the Bible, anyway? Are all parts of the Bible equally inspired?" I had no one to bring these questions to, and so they festered.

If I had kept my twisted view to myself, perhaps little harm would have come from it. But during a trip to the Manistee River I began to pass this view on to my little brother Bobby. It was early October, and a couple of my dad's friends had invited him along on a weekend trip north to try for king salmon. Fishing was never his favorite activity, but he would go now and then, especially when a group of his friends invited him. My brothers and I loved doing anything in the outdoors with him, though. So he asked his friends if they thought it would be all right if at least two of us came along, and they said that as long as he kept us out of their way, it would be fine. The salmon run was at its peak, and they expected to be busy.

Bobby and I watched as one or the other of my dad's friends fought a salmon for fifteen or twenty minutes and then held it proudly in the air for a picture. But every time one would pick up a fish from the gravel along the shore and hold it in the air, it would start to leak from what we had learned to call its "vent hole." The smaller ones, the ones that were silvery yet, leaked a creamy fluid.

"What's up with that?" Bobby asked. "It's leaking all over the place. Is that pee? It sure is not very clear. Maybe the fish is sick."

"No, no," said my dad, as his friends turned away to hide their laughter; "that's a male, and it's so exhausted from the fight that it's releasing its milt."

"Milt? What in the world is milt? It looks like milk. Is that what you mean?"

Since my dad and his friends were so busy putting the fish on a stringer and then getting their lines back into the river, I decided I should take my little brother aside and fill him in on everything I had learned in the last year or so about sexual reproduction. So I drew him back from the shore to some boulders where the guys had balanced their lanterns and started to introduce him to the strange new world I thought I had recently learned so much about.

"It'll seem awful strange at first, but the fact is that there are male and female fish, just like male and female people, boys and girls. That last fish was a male, and he was dropping sperm, or what Dad called milt. Those fatter ones, the ones that drop those little gold globules when they're held up, are the females. They're all coming up the river to spawn — they're going to try to make babies. If they're not caught, the females swish out a bed in the gravel with their tails. The males line up behind them and kind of jockey for prime position. When a female is ready, the male who is in the best position swims up next to her and kinda rubs against her. Then she drops her eggs into the gravel.

When she does that, he squirts out his sperm, and those little sperm swim around and try to find an egg to dig into. If the sperm get into eggs, pretty soon we get baby salmon."

Everything I had said was true, I'm pretty sure, but then I got into the part that was somewhat twisted: "It's a lot to take in all at once, I'm sure, but it's really a pretty neat way to go about this stuff. They don't really have private parts right out in plain sight that they have to worry about. The females do all the really hard work on the nest. Each male just has to fight other males off, something that's pretty cool anyways. Once they're in the bed together, they don't have to touch each other very much. Just a few little sideswipes from the male and the female drops her eggs. Then the male can go ahead and do his thing. First one, then the other. Just think about it: When you have your special assembly at school, ask yourself whether these fish might not have a better system than we do."

Concentrating as I was, I hadn't noticed that my dad, needing a couple of extra sinkers, had come up behind us to where all the spare tackle was stowed. He probably hadn't heard everything I had said, but it was clear that he had heard the last part. Right after I told Bobby about how great I thought the salmon system was, my dad cut in: "You trying to kid somebody, Bill? Don't you know Bobby is at a really tender time about the birds and bees and fish? You were too, once, you know, and probably not all that long ago. Where'd you get all these crazy ideas about sex, anyway?"

I couldn't admit that stuff I had seen and heard had scared me, not with all those men just a few feet away, so I only started to mumble something about hearing things from other kids in the bathroom at school.

But he cut me off: "Salmon sex is so great? The male and female don't care a stone about each other, they hardly even look each other in the eye, none of them gets any joy from opening up the mystery of one's body to another and trusting, they aren't sure if they ever have babies, and if they do, they couldn't tell theirs from any others. They get to spawn only once in their lives, and not too long after they spawn they start to break down and then it doesn't take long before they die and stink up the shoreline. You've got some serious things to get turned around in your life. And you sure don't want to be responsible for messing Bobby up about this stuff, do you?"

"I guess not."

And then Bobby's voice, from the side and overlapping my last words: "Don't get too worried, Dad. I learned my lesson a long time ago, the hard way. Whenever I fell for any of Bill's stories, I always got in big trouble. So I don't pay much attention to his jabber anymore." ◎

The Wall

Each fall I regularly drive down to The Wall and try to catch a steelhead. Strictly speaking, The Wall is a floodwall, a large concrete barrier along the east bank of the Grand River in downtown Grand Rapids, Michigan. The section of The Wall that I fish from is slightly downstream from the Sixth Street Dam, just on the edge of the Quarry Hole.

Before I made my very first trip to The Wall, I knew that I would be different from most of the other anglers there and might easily stand out among them. And although my concern might not have been fully rational, I worried about relating well enough to be able to learn from them what was working for steelhead.

The river forms one boundary — the most obvious boundary — of the city's west side. And many of the anglers along The Wall are west-siders; they find it easy to bike or even walk over to the river and cross the Sixth Street Bridge to find a place along The Wall, whipping their steelhead or salmon rods rhythmically in front of them on their way as if they were conducting such a large group of musicians that those in the percussion section needed special help to follow the beat.

Although the situation has been changing somewhat lately,

most west-siders are Polish and Roman Catholic. I am Dutch and Christian Reformed and grew up having frequent and almost frenzied arguments with my neighbor Peter Polaski about which one of what we called "our religions" was right.

We were only eleven or twelve at the time, and I would like to say that each of us knew a lot about and valued ecumenism or that we were motivated mainly by a deep and thorough concern for the other's spiritual health, but such statements would be lies. Each of us wanted to be right in every specific claim, and each of us wanted to win every overall argument, especially any argument about important topics like religion. Never since in my life have I been in such emotional arguments about religion; at that point I had not yet encountered what I now encounter regularly: a kind of mushy pluralism.

So Peter and I would blaze away at each other.

"What's with this praying to Mary, anyway?" I would say. "And worse, you sometimes pray to regular people that a bunch of monks in funny robes have decided are saints."

"At least we pray a lot," he came back, "and we're not afraid to let others know it. I've seen those sneaky little head bobs you call prayers before we eat when we have our block parties. It's like you're saying, 'Oh, please, please, don't let anybody know that I'm praying. I'm just clearing my throat and resting my eyes for a second here.'"

"Yeah, right, but I don't need to confess my sins to some priest in a smoky little booth. I can go right to God if I want to. We're connected."

"But do you ever confess anything? Most times you and your brothers walk around like you don't have a clue what sinning is. You seem to think that sinning is something that all the rest of us do but that you don't — oh no, not you, God's chosen people in wooden shoes, klomp, klomp, klomp!"

And on and on we would bicker, until at last we grew so angry and frustrated that we would either have to break into a fight or decide not to talk to each other for a couple of days.

So before I ever looked for a spot to stand along The Wall, I resolved to give no sign that I knew anything about religion. No references as I watched fish being landed to grace or mercy or blessings. No whistling along when the bells from St. Mary's echoed over the surface of the water in the early evening. Never an exclamation of "Lord God Almighty" or "Think of me now, Jesus" when a big fish porpoised near where I had just cast my lure. I didn't want differences in religion to start new arguments and thus stand in the way of my being able to learn what I needed to learn from my neighbors.

The same thing was true for differences in occupations. Most of the other guys fishing from The Wall came directly from blue-collar jobs, jobs for which steel-tipped boots, jeans with rolled-up cuffs, and light blue shirts with a name patch stitched on were standard attire. Some of them even showed up with a grimy grease rag sticking out of their hip pocket. And I could hear them cursing together about such things as rusty rotors, fouled plugs, misaligned dies, and jammed lathes.

I have a white-collar job. I usually wear wingtips, pleated pants, a dress shirt, and a striped tie to my job as a professor of English. When I am with colleagues, we talk about such things as how to diagram absolute phrases, how many spaces should follow a colon, and what role, if any, a writer's stated intention should play in hermeneutical practice.

I knew I could never bring up such topics while talking to

others along The Wall; such topics would only make them feel self-conscious or uneducated. I also knew that I couldn't wear any part of what I wore to teach as I was standing on The Wall. I had to find and wear some clothes that would keep me from sticking out. So I started wearing the splotchy jeans that I bought several years ago for painting around the house. I bought a Carhartt hooded sweatshirt from the local Salvation Army store; its shoulders have such pronounced scuffmarks that it looks as if someone once slept in it. And I wear an old pair of discount-store boots, the right one of which has its sole loose in the front so that about one inch of it flaps like a limp tongue.

But despite all my careful preparations, I still haven't been able to learn how nearly all of the other guys consistently catch steelhead while I am waiting to land my first. I know that steelhead are famous for being really difficult to catch. And I have heard on fishing shows that the bait one uses and the manner in which one presents it to steelhead have to be almost perfectly natural.

I must be doing something wrong. I did land a big moss-covered bullhead two years ago. And recently I fought a fish that I assumed was a steelhead, but I couldn't be sure since it fought its way into the heaviest current, thrashed off downstream, and tore the hook out of the flesh near its tail. Clearly, I could use some advice from all the successful anglers around me.

Advice, however, is something none of the others seems fully capable of giving. In any event, my attempts to foster something like a sustained conversation have so far been strikingly unsuccessful.

Once, for example, a guy approached me along the walkway

on top of The Wall and asked, "They hittin' pretty good down thisaway?"

"Yes," I responded, "from what I can see, they have been biting really well."

He flicked his cigarette into a foamy eddy and moved off along The Wall.

Another time a guy came up and asked whether the fisherman who had been reported to catch a sixteen-pound steelhead was the one who had been standing just a few feet down The Wall from me.

"Yes," I said, "it was he."

His eyes focused on mine for an instant; then he did a half-turn, leaned over slightly, put his index finger on the side of his nose, blew out a knotty string of mucous, and finally shuffled off.

If I am ever to get some advice, I will have to run into someone with sufficient linguistic resources to take more than a single short turn in a conversation.

As the season nears its end, I will continue for a while to go down and cast from The Wall. I will go even though I know I may never get any good advice. And I will go even though, as the chill in the wind sharpens and darkness takes a little more of each successive day by surprise, tying knots in fishing line becomes nearly impossible.

Anglers are creatures of perpetual hope, and I can only hope that the one whose bait presentation is accepted will, at last, be I. ☙

Bottom Feeders

O ne of my great comforts in life is fishing. And if I could have my way, I'd spend my fishing time amid the translucent green of alder bushes, working my way methodically from riffle to riffle in small streams feeding the Two-Hearted River near the Lake Superior coast of Michigan's Upper Peninsula, fishing for brook trout. As Robert Traver has written, pursuing trout is a wonderful experience since they "will not live, indeed cannot live, except where beauty dwells."

But as you can probably guess, I can't always fish where I would most like. I don't have enough disposable income to pay for frequent trips to the Upper Peninsula. Nor do I very often have enough time for such trips. I have letters of recommendation to write, all kinds of meetings to attend, papers to grade, students to advise, things to fix around the house, chores to do in the yard, oil in the car to change, and more. My life is not my own.

So when I am able to fish, I usually can't head up near the Two-Hearted but instead throw my equipment in the car, fight my way along the freeway, and end up casting from a concrete floodwall into the muddy water of the Grand River below the Sixth Street Dam in downtown Grand Rapids. In this world, you have to learn how to make compromises.

Fortunately for me, at certain times of the year good numbers of trout lie among the rocks below the dam. I'm not sure how much beauty they find as they come up the river skirting sunken tires and resting under bridges that have steel girders bleeding rust down the sides of concrete foundations, but they do come. In the spring, for instance, lots of steelhead come up the river from Lake Michigan looking for spawning gravel. And while many of these usually end up fanning out spawning beds in prettier streams entering the Grand farther upstream — the Rogue seems to be one of their favorites — quite a few stay below the dam. Maybe they, too, have somehow learned how to make compromises.

Standing on a floodwall in downtown Grand Rapids and tossing yarn flies or bucktail jigs for steelhead is not the same thing as standing near a gravel bar in an Upper Peninsula creek casting flies for brook trout, but one could do worse. Every once in a while as I cast from The Wall, I hook a steelhead, and the water erupts. The fish leaps and sends water droplets shimmering off in several directions simultaneously; it runs with the current until I can first slow it and then turn it; it frantically seeks submerged logs and boulders to try to wrap my line around; it thumps its head back and forth to send me the message along the line that it is thoroughly insulted that I managed to fool it, if only for a fateful split second; and all this time I'm mouthing silent prayers that my swivel will not tear open, my line will not snap, my drag will not jam, and I'll be able to enjoy the moment of conquest when I can ease the fish over the edge of my dropper net and let gravity and the flow of the current take it down into the cords.

Although such excitement can almost cause me to forget

that I am not fishing up north, there are two problems with fishing the Grand in the spring that keep reminding me where I am. The first is that, at that time of the year, steelhead are not the only fish in the river. In fact, the steelhead are just a regal minority among milling masses of various kinds of suckers, and most anglers will probably end up catching about six suckers to one steelhead. Some people think highly of suckers and can carry on for a long time about various ways to pickle them or smoke them or can them so that, in their words, "suckers can taste pretty good with saltines."

But to most people suckers are junk fish, and the thought of eating them would make their gorge rise. They are reacting, I guess, to what and how suckers usually feed. Suckers have a downward-pointing circle of a mouth, and with it they dredge their way along the bottom, vacuuming up such things as slugs and leeches and decaying body parts of dead crayfish. So, for example, if you fish with a jig and you let the jig rest for more than a few seconds on the bottom, you could easily find that a sucker has taken it in. When an exhausted sucker is hauled to the top of The Wall, usually its muckling circle of a mouth goes into a frenzied sucking spasm, apparently seeking something to attach itself to.

I am not as negative about suckers as most people are. Once hooked, they put up a fairly respectable fight, using the river currents to help them make strong runs downstream. However, I can't quite bring myself to eat those that I land. There's something about the image of their mouths' sucking spasms and about the sludge that I imagine them dredging up that makes it impossible for me to fire up the grill and slap some sides of sucker on it. I usually toss whatever suckers I catch into a five-gallon bucket and take them home for use in the backyard. In a garden or a flowerbed, they make great fertilizer.

The other problem about fishing the Grand involves street people. Just three or four feet from the edge of the floodwall that I fish from, behind the guardrail, stand some refuse barrels placed at intervals of twenty yards or so by the city's Parks and Recreation Department. Those who fish generally use these barrels for their knotted or twisted line, the cardboard and plastic packages their lures came in, and the worms and leeches and minnows that no longer have enough wiggle in them to serve as bait. They also use these barrels for whatever they've brought along to eat or drink and no longer want. Into these barrels, then, go cast-off items such as pop cans with a little bit of liquid sluicing around inside them, bags of potato chips with a few crumbs still in the bottom, and the wrappers of fruit pies with some of the cherry or blueberry filling smeared on them.

Just about the time when it gets hard to see where in the river lures land when they are cast, various street people come shuffling along the top of the floodwall — it always seems to me that they simply materialize in the twilight — competing with one another for the right to rummage through the stuff in the barrels in the hopes of finding fruit pie filling they can lick off wrappers or scraps of potato chips that they can wipe onto a moistened finger and then bring to their mouths. After drinking the liquid in pop cans and licking around the pop-tops, they generally save the cans so that they can turn them in for the deposit and then buy a quart of beer or a bottle of some cheap red wine.

I guess there's nothing wrong with their helping themselves to this stuff from the trash. It's just that if I happen to be standing near a barrel, somebody hanging around only a few feet away from me while pawing his or her way through the junk in the barrel can make me pretty tense, especially as the sun gets close to dropping behind the hills on the west side of the city. There's a fine line, you know, between helping oneself to some trash in a barrel and asking for or demanding money or food from a fisherman standing nearby trying to catch a steelhead. The fear I carried was always of what might happen if they were really hungry and they weren't able to find much edible trash in a barrel.

Yet I never had any real trouble from any of these street people until a recent spring. Fairly late one Saturday night in early April, just as I was about to leave the river and head home, an older man edged his way along the guardrail toward the barrel to my left. He dug around in the barrel for a minute, examining a few wrappers closely before dropping them back, and then he succumbed for a few seconds to spasms of high and dry wheezings. Once he could breathe without convulsing, he crossed the line. He talked directly to me: "Hey, man, can't you help me out a little?"

I gave him one quick glance over my shoulder and then turned back to face the water. But that glance left me with two images that can still worm their way into my consciousness if I'm not on guard. The first is of his hat, something like a cheap copy of an aviator's hat, a hat with earflaps, red flannel earflaps standing out at odd angles from the sides of his face. The other is of the left side of his face, where either a fire or a birth defect or something had left him with a mass of splotchy, cranberry-colored flesh hanging somewhat limply between his mouth and his ear.

As much as I had always been aware that one of these street

people might someday shift attention from a trash barrel to me, I didn't know exactly how to respond to this guy. I knew I wasn't going to haul my wallet out and let him start wondering how much money I was carrying around. Then I had it: I remembered that I had already caught several suckers. I could give this guy a sucker, maybe even the biggest one. But better yet, the voice of generosity within me nudged, go the extra mile and give him all seven of the suckers you've caught so far. So I ended up handing over all my suckers. "They're best if you put them in the smoker for several hours, maybe even overnight," I told him. I even tossed in the plastic bucket so that he could fairly comfortably carry what had to add up to be around fifteen to twenty pounds of fish.

The guy took the pail and moved off along The Wall. He never said thanks; he never said a thing. But that was all right; I suspected that he didn't have a lot of practice reacting to gifts.

The next day we had an interesting sermon on how God used some of the experiences of the Israelites as slaves in Egypt to lay the foundation for laws recorded in Deuteronomy. While standing around enjoying strawberry shortcake and punch during the fellowship time after the service, I made my own practical connection to the sermon by telling several of my friends how just the night before I had managed to act pretty generously in a situation that had plenty of potential for being ugly.

"You gave him all the fish?" Mark wondered. "And the bucket too? Aren't you afraid of having given away too much, of leading that guy to watch for you and single you out each time you go down there, of making him expect more and more?"

"Nah, nah, nah," I replied. "In that situation, it was the least I could do." ⑥

Clear and Pure

I don't fish to live, but if you were to catch me in a somewhat unguarded moment, you might get me to admit that I very nearly live to fish. If this seems somewhat excessive or clearly wrong, I should point out that in this respect I am not alone. I know people who become so irritable if they haven't fished in a week or two that their spouses banish them to the garage, where they put on their fishing vests and hats and sit in their trailered boats lubricating reels, honing hooks, and studying the undulating lines on hydrographic maps. I also know people who pay more attention to weather maps showing the precise location of cold fronts and to charts predicting the best fishing times in upcoming months than they do to their children's dates of birth and to their own wedding anniversaries. People like this, some critics say, have a kind of disease.

Maybe so, but what attracts me to fishing is different from what attracts many other people. When they describe why they love to fish, their descriptions descend into murky and mysterious depths. Norman Maclean, for one, writes of looking in rivers for special rocks, those rocks on which are timeless raindrops and under which are words. Some of my friends talk of their fascination with contemplating the wavering line deep in the water of lakes where blue-green shades off into black. Other friends talk of the almost feverish anticipation they feel as they wait to see what the dark water of deep holes on rivers will surrender to them. All these people miss the mark.

What is great about fishing has to do with clarity: Do a certain thing at a certain time in a certain way in a certain place under certain weather conditions and you will catch a certain kind of fish. All this talk about lobbing out bait, hoping to catch some kind of fish, having no idea what kind that might be, squealing with delighted surprise upon actually catching something — all this talk about dumb luck or natural caprice or unwavering patience — is the babble of the ignorant.

Go down below the Sixth Street Dam on the Grand River in Grand Rapids in April just after a mild rain, use a long rod and a spinning reel with a smooth drag, run your main line to one eye of a three-way swivel, attach a six-inch length of four-pound line to the second of the eyes of the swivel and fasten two medium-sized sinkers high on that line near the swivel, attach a four-foot length of six-pound fluorocarbon line as your leader to the third of the eyes of the swivel, on the end of that leader use a number twelve hook as your terminal tackle and hide it inside a floating spawn sack, make quartering casts upstream and allow the spawn sack to slip downstream just above the rocks and at precisely the speed of the current below the surface, and you will catch steelhead.

Or go out after midnight some humid night in late August to the breakwaters channeling the Muskegon River into Lake Michigan, take about a seven-foot graphite rod with a spinning or baitcasting reel, use eight-pound test line to which you tie a number-nine silver Rapala minnow bait without using any kind of snap or swivel, add one number-four sinker to the line about four feet above the Rapala, use an electric motor to troll just fast enough to make the minnow bait wiggle along the edge of the boulders on the side of the breakwater, occasionally snap the rod forward so that the Rapala darts erratically, and you will catch walleye.

In fact, if you learn enough to do the right thing whenever you fish, you will catch whatever kind of fish you want to catch. That is what I mean by clarity. Such clarity is pure, it is elegant, it is crystalline, it is unambiguous and uncompromising. Such clarity is possible only in a world that can be understood and subdued.

The main — really, the only — problem I ever had with fishing had to do with a day of the week: Sunday. I never really knew if on Sunday it would be all right for me to fish. I do know that currently those who attend our church on Sunday mornings do all sorts of different things once church is over. I have some friends who use Sunday afternoons to wash and wax their cars and mow and edge their lawns. I have other friends who drive for an hour or so to play golf at courses they've read reviews of in the newspaper. And one of my friends sought out an early-morning service at another church so that he could say that he went to church before he took his family down to Detroit to watch the Lions play.

Thinking of these practices always made me pretty uneasy. The most I was ever able to let myself do on Sunday besides going to church and listening to soft music was to take a short walk. But I never looked around all that much; I generally kept my head down and guarded my thoughts. Even so, I always experienced little flashes of guilt.

The trouble started for me when I was a child. My mother grew up in a church in which, although there were about eight hundred members, only eight or nine men, all of them elders, had the confidence to say that they were probably saved. Those eight or nine elders were the only ones who ever took Communion; they walked to the front of the church while all the others watched. And those eight or nine, I suppose, were the only ones who didn't flinch when the minister railed — as he frequently did — about rank sinners and a righteous God. Most people who grew up in this church worked hard to find out as much as they could about how to live a holy and consecrated life. And then they worried about how far they inevitably would fall short. They must have been well acquainted with holy terror.

After my mother married my father, she left that church, but that church never entirely left her. She had breathed too long the filtered air of strict Sabbatarianism. So when I was really young, her views about how to observe the Sabbath made Sunday a very grim day for me. I have memories of not being able to go outside and play baseball with the Catholic kids from down the street; they had gone to Saturday-night Mass and had the whole Sunday free for whatever they wanted to do — including standing outside our living room window hooting at me. Baseball? Play? Enjoy myself? "Not on Sunday," my mother would warn, asking, "What do you suppose God thinks of those who know what he wants and then ignore it? Hasn't he set aside a place for them?" I stayed inside, but all the time I alternated between feeling sorry for myself and worrying about my friends.

I also have memories of not being able to change out of my church clothes for at least the early part of the day; I was supposed to sit in these good clothes and read or listen to the radio and think of matters related to my soul. But most of all I have memories of lots of bad headaches. Sometimes they would start already on Saturday night.

Now that I am older, I no longer get those headaches as often, but until recently I would regularly confront a painful dilemma: Each week there was Sunday, especially Sunday afternoon, with its hours free of pressing commitments, its hours that I could use to restore my spirit, its hours that would line up respectfully yet insistently and murmur questions to me about whether spending them fishing would necessarily be a sin.

Recently I worked my way toward a reasoned response. I began by noting the fact that I had already started to take walks on Sunday afternoons. For those I usually wore my jogging shoes, but occasionally because of snow and slush I had to wear my hiking boots. My hiking boots were not that much different from the boots of my waders — both sets of boots were heavy, brown, and cleated. It was sometimes pretty tough walking through the resistance of the snow and slush, a resistance that was not significantly different from the resistance one felt wading through the water of a river. When I walked in the woods, I often used a walking stick; this too was not significantly different from my wading stick. Finally, the floppy hat that I almost invariably wore while walking was in fact the same hat that I wore while fishing. Therefore, I concluded, if I on Sunday afternoons could justify walking along sidewalks or paths in the woods, I could justify walking along river bottoms. The fact that I would carry and occasionally use a fishing rod could be seen as incidental.

So one Sunday in a recent September, right when the king salmon were making their run from Lake Michigan up the rivers of Michigan, I decided to head down to the rapids below the Sixth Street Dam. Since I had so much of the day to work with, I decided to wade, not just cast from The Wall, as I had always done when I had only an hour or two. I had packed all my gear in the car the night before, and it was only prudent, I thought, to wait to leave until most of my neighbors were probably settled into their Sunday-afternoon naps. Thus by the time I got down to the river, the parking lot was almost full, dozens of people were already in the river, and seventy-five or a hundred spectators were leaning over the concrete wall around the fish ladder pointing as the salmon thrashed their way from one small holding pool up to the next. I skirted the crowd, eased my way into the water while bracing myself against the trough of especially strong current along the west side, and waded across most of the river so that I could stand near the edge of the Quarry Hole on the opposite side.

That afternoon I had supremely good fishing. Using a dropper rig, I would toss a yellow yarn ball with an orange dot in the middle about fifteen yards out in front of me and reel slowly as the current took it through the deepest part of the hole. Just as the yarn ball would begin to turn and rise near the end of the drift, a salmon would take it.

Strike after strike after strike. Hooked fish were swirling powerfully on the surface and making determined runs with the currents, those fishing downstream from me were scrambling to get out of the way as I staggered among the rocks trying to chase fish downstream, spectators along the bank were shouting to their kids and pointing in my direction, I was struggling to keep the sweat out of my eyes and pry hooks out of bony mouths and cut off frayed line and check on knots and keep my drag adjusted properly and smooth out the kinks that developed in my line and make sure that the safety belt around the top of my waders was tight and above all watch out that I didn't slip off any moss-covered rock and fill my waders with water.

I wasn't able to keep track of how many salmon I fought that afternoon. I do know that for hours after I stepped out of the river my right forearm and the small of my back ached from having to pull back and put pressure on so many fish. Those few hours had to be among the best of my life.

By the time I stepped out of the river and walked back to my car, I was throwing a long shadow. The street I usually took to get back to the freeway was blocked off for repair, so I had to cut through downtown Grand Rapids to head home. Sixth Street to Monroe, Monroe to Louis, up the slant on Louis to Fulton, Fulton for half a block to Division, and then south. Just where Division intersects Cherry I had to stop for a red light. On the northeast corner of that intersection, just on the edge of the circle of light thrown by a streetlight, she stood. Spiked red heels showing some toe cleavage, a delicately braided gold bracelet on each ankle, and from there on up her legs purple Lycra

Spandex, Spandex so tight that it cast the muscles of her calves and especially those along her thighs into exquisite relief.

It was there that my eyes lingered.

But no! Oh, gracious Heavens, no! — I wrenched my eyes away, glanced up to the traffic light, realized that the light was already green, and then hit the gas so abruptly that the car lurched once and then roared away from the intersection toward home. "No! No! No!" I repeated to myself. "I can't be a part of this!"

By the time I was a couple of miles south on Division, I had settled down enough to begin formulating an explanation and justification. In retrospect, it was clear to me that the look had not been fully intentional; it was certainly more of a reflex than anything else, and who can be responsible for every last physical reflex? If a muscle twitches, can you tell it to stop? Furthermore, the look had obviously not lasted long at all; if it had been measured, it would almost surely have been measured in milliseconds. Further still, it had clearly been only a look; no other of my senses had come into play. Plus the image that the look produced could surely be of little danger. To the best of my knowledge, no one has ever made a convincing case that an image by itself can affect attitudes or values. And I had never heard any minister say that carrying around such an image was a sin. What one did with the image, possibly, but not just happening to have it in your memory.

By late the next day, I had succeeded in taking all such logical points and using them to erect an elaborate system, such an impressive system, in fact, that I was fully at peace. It was clear to me that I had come through the Sunday-night incident on Division Street pure and undefiled. Developing the system had demanded more than a trifling amount of work, however. I noted that I was fortunate to live in the world that I did live in; I knew I would not want to grow old and face any loss of strength in a world where I could not be certain that such effort as I had expended would lead to such clarity as I had achieved. ⑥

In the Dark

Each autumn, I take a trip that makes my friends wonder about my judgment and worry about my safety. I head north, the direction that since childhood I have most deeply associated with creation and recreation, all the way to the Manistee River below Tippy Dam.

I avoid the pattern set by many anglers, those who rise around 5:00 a.m., kick Thermos bottles over on the driveway as they load their pick-ups, drive off through veils of fog, and stop an hour or so later at some Hilltop Bakery for an apple fritter. Instead, I leave in the late afternoon, two hours or so after schools get out for the day.

Since Tippy Dam is about two hours north of Grand Rapids, by the time I arrive the sun has been almost entirely eclipsed by the irregular line of forested hills to the west, leaving only nearly horizontal slants of light to turn the tops of the oaks along the south rim of the river valley the reddish side of gold. Each year I struggle with the emotion, but each year I can't help but feel ambivalent about these sunsets: almost a giddy awe in view of the trees' burnished crowns, but some dull, aching misgivings as well. For as the sun's rays burn higher and higher into the oaks, it means that the walkway down to the river, where I hope to find the king salmon spawning run at its peak, is increasingly succumbing to implacable darkness.

The descent to the river is the first of the challenges that I face because I choose to start fishing at dusk and continue through most of the night. Those who have trekked into canyons out west would probably scoff at any suggestion that the walk down to a river in the Midwest might be dangerous. And I must admit that it is not far from the valley rim to the edge of the water, probably only a quarter mile or so. Further, the trail is not truly steep; the rim is probably less than two hundred vertical feet above the river. Further still, the trail is paved with either concrete or asphalt for most of the way and has many steps (I always lose count above 150) laid in along its course.

But these steps are not uniformly wide, so as I move deeper into the dark I cannot predict exactly where their edges are. Worse, many of these edges have been rounded off by thousands of boots over the years. And worst of all, as successful anglers drag salmon up the trail on stringers, the females drop thousands of translucent orange eggs, and the males release ounces of milt all over the walkway. At the top of the steps, I am always pleased to see this cold stew, for it means that there are salmon in the river and that they are biting, but I know that, unless I edge my way down the steps as cautiously as one tests ice on a spring-fed lake, my feet will go skating out from under me and I will risk cracking my tailbone.

If I manage to get down the steps without suffering anything worse than a cramp in the muscles above my knees or in my wrists — one hand trying to control my fishing rod and net and tackle and lantern and raincoat, the other alternating between clinging to and sliding down the handrail next to the walkway — I can stash my spare tackle on the bank, light my lantern and build a little cairn to balance it on, and start looking for a good place to wade into the river.

Even in the limited light of the lantern, I can usually find a sand spit or gravel bar that angles into the river. These extend out to fairly secure places to stand. It's after I hook a big fish that I face really serious problems with footing.

Many of the bigger kings, especially if they are fresh from Lake Michigan, seem, when hooked, to consider it nothing more than playful romping to make runs of over a hundred yards downstream from the angler. If you have a reel that holds hundreds of yards of line and that has a dependable drag, you can try to hold your place in the currents and hang on while the fish bores away farther and farther back toward the big lake. Soon, you hope, you will be able to tire it, turn its head, and pump it back upstream to your net.

Reels that can hold that much line are too heavy for me to fish with through most of the night. So after any fish I hook charges off seventy-five or eighty yards away from me, I have to start chasing it or it will pull all the line off my spool. Staggering along downstream in strong currents with only wavering streaks of light from lanterns on the shore to guide me, all the while trying to hold my rod high and to peer ahead for an inkling of what I might be stepping into, is not the safest thing I do in life.

More than once I have swung a foot forward into the side of a rock, usually losing my balance, lurching around desperately, trying to keep water from seeping or spilling over the top of my waders.

My most dangerous pursuit ever took me near an old birch

that had been blown into the river and now lay with its branches steadily sawing the current. At the time I had no way of knowing it, but two guys fishing just downstream from the birch had tied a stringer to one of its outermost branches, and on this stringer they had secured four or five kings. These fish were lying resignedly in a little pool below the branch when I tried to plant a boot across several of their backs. I assume that they were not happy about having the nylon cord of the stringer threaded through their lower jaws and about being forced to lie side by side in the pool. I know that when I tried to make room for my boot among them, they were not pleased.

If they had been some other kind of fish, cute little slivers of six- or eight-inch perch, for example, all I would have felt would have been some fluttering around my ankle. But these were kings, kings that weighed twenty pounds or more, and their sudden thrashing knocked me off balance. I was able to arrest my fall, but to do so I had to jam my knee against the sharp edge of a large rock. I didn't break or separate anything, but for nearly three months afterwards I carried an uncomfortable but iconic reminder of my misstep in the river — water on that knee.

It doesn't really make sense, since missteps in rivers that can fill waders with water occasionally lead to drownings, but what I fear even more than missteps while fishing at night is other anglers' backcasts. One of the attractions of fishing at night is that the river is usually not as crowded with anglers as during the day. But the fish do not distribute themselves evenly throughout the river, and experienced anglers have an extra sense that alerts them to where others are hooking fish, so some congregating of anglers in certain spots is inevitable.

Imagine, then, four or five guys standing within several feet of one another, imagine further that they are all using rods about nine feet long, imagine further still that they whip these behind them to get the momentum they need to cast their lures well out into the river, and imagine finally that all of them have at least one ultra-sharp hook at the end of the line they whip back and then snap forward.

The sound of rods and lines whipping the air is, I find, eerily entrancing. But if anglers do not check the spaces behind and around them before making their backcasts, they can drive a hook into a fellow angler's flesh. What a flashing hook can do to parts of the human body is, without exception, ugly.

So far I have never been hooked. The closest I came was when a guy took my hat off shortly after he moved from backcast into cast. A little whup, some rustling of my hair, a sudden touch of cold, and my hat disappeared into the dark. His string of apologies made it more difficult for me to forget how narrowly I had skirted the pain.

I have, however, seen three other fishermen with hooks in their bodies. One of them had one of the treble hooks of a Mepps spinner in the well-defined muscles of his left forearm. Fortunately, when the careless angler first felt his lure hit the other's forearm, he gave a sharp jerk on his line. Thus, the hook didn't just enter the man's forearm — it entered, bore a neat arc through the muscle, and emerged, barb and all, about a half-inch lower on his arm. After realizing what had happened, the victim took out his pliers, cut the barb and point of the hook off, held the hook by its shank, and wiggled it backwards out of his arm.

Another victim wasn't as fortunate. He had been hooked in

one of the muscles along the back of his neck, just above the collar of his wool shirt. In his case, the point and barb of the hook had penetrated the muscle and stayed there. So one of his friends had to try a different method of extraction. He bent the eye of the hook down toward his friend's neck, thereby rounding off and putting pressure on the curve of the hook. He then took some of his heaviest fishing line and looped it under that curve. Finally, while maintaining pressure on the hook with his left hand, he wrapped the ends of the line around several fingers of his right hand and gave the line a sharp yank. He tore up the tissue of his friend's neck a bit, but the hook pulled out, giving off just the slightest slurping sound.

A third victim needed assistance that he trusted no one at the dam to provide. He had the hook of a half-ounce Little Cleo spoon in his nose, about half an inch up on the left side. The barb of the hook had not emerged from his flesh, so it was impossible to cut the point and barb off and work the rest of the hook backward out of his nose. And everyone could see that the curves of his nose and cheek allowed no good angle to put pressure on the shank of the hook to prepare for a fishing-line yank. So after glancing skeptically at nearby anglers, some of whom were pulling rusty jackknives and bloodstained tweezers out of their vests, this man decided to drive twenty miles to a clinic in Manistee. As he packed up his gear and headed toward the steps, the lure, hanging down along the side of his mouth, clearly fulfilled the promise of its nickname: the "Wigl" lure.

Even in the face of such actual or potential troubles, I will continue to make these excursions, at least until I fear I cannot climb back up from the river to my car. Why?

It is not that night fishing lets me get by using heavier line than anyone would use during the day. It is not that in the dark the salmon feel secure enough to roam more widely in the river. It is not even that at night many of them are quite aggressive biters. It has to do, ultimately, with mystery, struggle, and revelation.

When a king salmon takes my lure at night, it usually does so far out of my sight. Once hooked, it will often jump or thrash violently on the surface, maybe thirty or forty yards away from me, and the anglers closest to the small storm in the water will yell, sometimes with some anxiety or impatience in their voices, "Whose fish?"

"Mine," I yell, "way over here," and I know that although they might have a chance to glimpse the fish, it will stay hidden from me.

If it's a big fish, it will often start making runs away from me. Usually it will head downstream, but if it's feeling somewhat imperious, it will reverse its direction and head back upstream, moving with strength even against the current. Once upstream from me, it can circle around and start to head downstream behind my back. But I never see it; all I can do is turn and try to focus on the point where the line slices the surface of the river.

Even after I begin to wear the fish down and start to inch toward the shoreline, with the fish sometimes boiling around in the shallow water only a few yards from my feet, it is too dark for me to make it out.

And so for minute after minute, my forearms cramping from pulling back on the rod, the small of my back aching from bending backwards to exert more pressure against the fish, my feet knocking into rocks around me, I never get to see what's on the end of the line.

Only when I succeed at last in hauling it up on the gravel of the shoreline do I have a chance to see what I've caught. Then, using the beam from my small flashlight to cut narrowly through the dark, I suck breath sharply past my teeth when I realize that what I have held fast to and wrested from the dark and swirling swiftness — its eyes intent on the spawn, glinting with knowledge of life in death — is clearly a thing of beauty. And we all know what that is. ☉

Too Good to Be True?

A second or two after I had hooked a smallmouth bass on each of four consecutive casts, a part of my mind that I often struggle to subdue raised the oily question of whether something this wonderful could really be happening to me.

It was not that I was fishing a poor piece of water. The eddy under a partially blown-over cottonwood about a hundred yards below a dam on the Flat River could have been featured in a fishing video — it was deep, it had a set of pronounced current breaks, it lay in the shade for much of the day, and it was full of large rocks that the bass could use for cover.

Nor was it that I didn't have an effective lure. The diving minnow I was using — my only lure that ran deep enough to reach the bottom of the pool — would knock its way erratically through the rocks, and as it caromed off one rock or another, the bass made me think they were competing to hit it.

Nor was it even that I was unaware that people in real life sometimes caught fish on consecutive casts. My friend Arnie had often told me how in a bay of Lake Michigan southeast of Waugoshance Point he had once caught over thirty smallmouth bass in a row while casting to the shady side of some boulders the size of Volkswagens.

So it's not really that I thought of such fishing as impossible. But on my fifth cast my lure went sailing into the branches of the cottonwood, where it hung tangled around branches with arthritic-looking knobs and joints. There it remained, clearly in my line of sight and obviously out of my reach. A few yanks on the line — first tentatively, then forcefully — only made the branches sway slightly and ultimately snapped my line.

So there I was, up to my waist in the current, lacking a lure that could get deep enough for the fish, and facing the challenge of figuring out how fine motor control in my right hand and arm could operate in total disregard of my conscious will.

On the slog downstream back to the bridge where I had parked, I began to suspect that only a steady and severe emphasis on particular elements of the ethnic and religious traditions from and into which I grew could have been powerful and insidious enough to make my hand and arm do what parts of my brain wanted to avoid.

When I was a child, I would often fool around with my brothers — "hunyocking" we called it, teasing, tattling, taunting. As the noise intensified, some close relative — usually a female relative — would try to scare us into quieting down by intoning, "Laughing now? Crying in a minute!" Even as a child I used to wonder why crying had to follow laughing and, at that, follow it almost immediately.

As I grew older and occasionally found myself being swept into convulsive laughter, I never once heard a relative exult, "Laugh! Don't stop! What a magnificent sound!" Usually I heard something like, "Bill, you better watch it. If you don't stop now, you know you'll choke or get the hiccups. You might even give yourself one of those bad headaches that everybody on the one side of the family gets."

Now when I sit in our faculty conference room during a break, people will walk by, overhear the boisterous talk and laughter, and then poke their heads in to scold: "It sounds like you're having way too much fun in here!" Colleagues regale one another with tales of vacation and convention trips, and then they catch themselves, pause, and say, "It was so much fun it almost had to be sinful!"

I even occasionally hear people who are lacerated with tragedies within their families say things like, "We should have expected something horrible to happen. Things had been going so well for so long. It just couldn't last." *hmmm. Many of the sentiments @ the funeral*

As I plowed a vanishing furrow through the water back to my car, I concluded that it must be possible for such a view of life to worm its way into parts of the brain we are not conscious of, or even into the control centers of muscle cells.

Things got confusing, though, when on the drive home from the Flat I recalled other fishing excursions. A particularly puzzling one was a trip a few years earlier to Lake Erie for walleye with my colleague Ken and several of his friends.

As our chartered boat settled off the rough lake into the calm of the channel at the end of the day, Ken lolled in a deck chair, pretended to light an enormous cigar, tossed his head back, and said, "What a beautiful day! Life is so good. A gift. God's gracious gift."

What was puzzling was that this was the same man who

only an hour or so earlier could not even stand on his own to reel in a three-pound walleye. The waves were four to five feet high, and despite an alert and skilled captain, the boat occasionally drifted sideways to the waves, where it would wallow sickeningly. But the most important factor was that Ken had already spent several years fighting amyloidosis, the disease that everyone knew would kill him sooner or later, and his muscles were largely wasted now, thin cords taut between his joints.

So when it was Ken's turn to move to the stern and reel in a fish, I had to kneel beside him, bracing one knee against the wall at the stern and a foot against a locker to my right, grabbing Ken by the belt that now went around his waist one and one-half times. As the boat pitched and wallowed, I shifted my weight to keep my grip on Ken's belt. "Young man," he coughed out, "don't you dare let go of me! This fish is coming to me; I'm not going to the fish!"

After Josh, the first mate, netted the fish, Ken and I collapsed in the eighth of an inch or so of bloody water sloshing around on the deck, both exhausted, I from straining to keep my balance and to stop Ken from falling down or pitching into the lake, he from standing and turning the crank of a well-greased fishing reel.

Since I was only getting to know Ken at the time, I did not understand how someone who had spent most of the day being taunted by reminders of how much strength he had lost, and the end of the day sitting in wet and bloodstained pants, could still think of the day as one of God's good gifts.

After Ken died, hundreds of his former students testified that they will never forget Robert Frost's line "Nature's first green is gold," primarily because of the spring semester when Ken took their class outside, read the poem to them as loudly as he could manage, and then sent them to find some first gold on campus, examine it closely, and record their reactions in their journals. For many, Frost's line was the emblem of Ken's profound effect on their lives.

At the same time, some close readers of the poem quietly wondered about this response. "True," they said, "that line is and points to a thing of beauty. But look how the poem goes down from there: leaf to leaf, Eden to grief, dawn to day. And did students ever think about the last line, which also serves as the title — 'Nothing gold can stay'?"

I had been one of Ken's students in a fall semester, not during the spring, so when I heard such comments, I was a bit reluctant to respond. Still, by the time Ken died, I had gotten to know him well, so I think I can now describe some of the ways in which he was trying to change students with this poem. Mostly, he wanted to get students into the habit of noticing, of paying attention, of working to see. And for Ken, the gold, I am sure, even if it lasted only an hour, was nevertheless for that hour essentially beautiful. Springtime's budding out foreshadowed for him a final fuller flowering.

A couple of weeks after my lure had begun its life of hanging out in the cottonwood, I returned to that eddy, later in the day than last time but armed this time with several minnow baits that would dive down deep and knock through the rocks.

I fished the pool thoroughly: I pitched the lure under the branches and then ran it through the depths at all kinds of angles. But I didn't have a single hit. Disappointed and a little confused, I eased away from the edge of the eddy, and as I did so I heard noises from upstream. Thirty or forty feet away, almost in the middle of the dangerous whirlpool below the dam, dozens of huge smallmouth bass were splashing around feeding on something on the surface.

The water they were in, I knew, was too deep to wade in safely, but I also knew that several rock bars led off at various angles from shallow water into the pool. If I probed along these, I might find one that extended far enough to allow me to cast to the fish. Once in position, I would have to figure out what the bass were feeding on and then experiment with lures in hopes of finding one that came close to matching their prey. I was not brimming with hope.

As I snugged up the safety belt on my waders before edging off along my first rock bar, I wondered what Ken would say about the challenge that these smallmouth bass had seemingly conspired to present.

At first there were no words, only an image: a memory of the picture of himself that Ken had mounted on the wall of our departmental conference room as a joke prior to the party for his early retirement. There he was, his head cocked to the right, a grin so large and lopsided that it was pulling his face off center to the left, and an unlit Cuban cigar in his hand. After the image came words I took to be his: "Young man, you know very well this is a gift. Not the gift you came here expecting, but a gift nevertheless. You don't really mean to tell me you need help unwrapping a gift meant especially for you, do you?" ⑥

The Path of the Wind

B ack in the mid-1950s (whenever my sons hear me using phrases like that, they ask me what it was like when the last of the dinosaurs died), back, that is, when I was six years old, the stretch of pitted concrete linking two sections of the main loop on the far north side of the camping area at Grand Haven State Park had no official or unofficial street signs but was commonly known as Diaper Alley.

This name was very confusing for me. My mom always told me to cover my ears and look away whenever we heard anyone using what she called "potty words." Then, with a facial expression mixing sadness, scorn, and condemnation, she would sigh, "Filthy mouths, absolutely filthy — where does it say we're supposed to think of these things?" And if any word ever belonged among the potty words, I thought, surely *diaper* did. *Diaper, double diapers, rubber pants, training pants, wipes* — weren't they all potty words? But in the campground at Grand Haven, everyone, even the park rangers, called the section of the park where my family was camping for a week Diaper Alley.

They did so, of course, because all of the families who were foolish, desperate, or brave enough to camp with babies and toddlers were automatically assigned to campsites along this noisy and sometimes noisome stretch of pavement. The park managers apparently wanted to keep all the whimpering and crying and screaming — as well as the all-too-audible parental responses — confined within one small section of the park.

We were camping with my mom's side of the family. Uncle Gerald and Aunt Gerry had three boys and a girl, the youngest boy only ten months old. Uncle Arie and Aunt Hattie had two young girls, the younger one just learning to put two or three steps together before wobbling and then collapsing onto her well-cushioned bottom, each time looking newly startled and betrayed. And we had been assigned a site on the Alley because of my baby brother, Bruce, who tried not to wear anything more than a diaper and who had a lot of trouble keeping that diaper up. Since the grandpa whom I didn't remember but whom I was supposed to resemble in several uncanny ways had died more than five years earlier, Grandma Fannie stayed with one of her children's families one year, a different one the next, and the third one after that.

Although I was confused, even embarrassed, by what I had to say whenever anyone asked me where in the park my family was camping, Diaper Alley had one great advantage for me. At the state park, ᴛ could have been drawn to the swimming beach, and when I got a few years older and a friend taught me the trick of using a squirt gun to shoot cold water onto the backs of girls who had undone their bikini tops while sunning on their stomachs, I often found myself on the beach, totally unaware that the sun was burning into my light skin various kinds of payment-due notices that I would have to honor, with interest, when I got older. I could have been drawn to the concession stand, where attendants whirled strands of cotton candy into

large and intricate bouffants and then flourished them tantaliz-
ingly before young kids who had sand-coated coins clasped in
their hands. I could have been drawn to the sets of monkey bars
erected on the edges of the campground, where kids of various
ages egged one another into trying flips and somersaults into
sand, all of them seeing how close to breaking their necks they
could come without ever really hurting themselves. But since
our notorious alley was on the north side of the camping area,
it was near the walkway along the channel for the Grand River
as it entered Lake Michigan. And the walkway led directly out to
the south pier.

When I was six, if someone had asked me where I would
like to spend the rest of my life, I would have said that I wanted
to use the railing of the walkway as the crossbeam of a lean-to
fort I would build, roll out my sleeping bag and the tattered
remnant of my baby blanket, find a place nearby to stash my
Mickey Mantle and Al Kaline baseball cards, store some bottles
of Nehi Grape and a package or two of Oreos in a cooler, and
live on the walkway to the pier at Grand Haven.

In part this was because just a few yards from the walkway
stood one of the best bait houses I had ever seen. The whole interior was moist, dripping. Along the walls stood concrete tanks
as high as my chest, each of them occasionally overflowing with
bitingly cold water. Running along the wall just above the back
of the tanks was a pipe with high-pressure nozzles at regular intervals; these sent tight streams of water drilling into the surface
of the water in the tanks. When I stood on tiptoe, I could see that
the tanks were full of minnows, dense subsurface swirlings of
dart-like shapes, so numerous that I thought you could dip a net
into them forever and never come up without a wriggling mass.

I would have been perfectly content spending much of each day nosing around in that bait house — and the various attendants never seemed to mind having me around, as long as I didn't try to grab minnows or get in the way of customers — but what was even more intriguing to me was what the customers used the minnows for. They would come into the bait house with various kinds of containers, from tidy little quart pails to clunky five-gallon buckets, some made of Styrofoam, some of plastic, some of aluminum. And they would buy three dozen or six dozen or a dozen dozen minnows, 50¢ a dozen, three dozen for $1.49.

Then they carried the minnows out on the pier and used them for bait. I didn't know exactly how they were rigging those minnows up, since my dad and mom had composed a short chorus to the effect that I was never to go out on that pier, a pier without guardrails, without an adult accompanying me, but what I did know was that those who returned from the pier returned with perch, lots of perch.

These were not the stunted creatures schooling along the bottoms of all too many lakes these days, four- or five-inch slivers of yellow and brown, fish that sometimes bite on lures nearly as big as themselves and then make you wonder whether you have anything on the line. These were perch as they were meant to be, twelve or fourteen or sixteen inches long, fish with deep bellies and some breadth in the shoulders, fish that some of the anglers said almost "filleted themselves."

And the anglers brought them back in amazing numbers. Some filled five-gallon buckets and then used Radio Flyers or two-wheelers to transport them. Some put their perch on a stringer, got help heaving the stringer over their shoulder, and came off the pier with dozens and dozens of perch slapping around all the way down to their ankles.

As I stood by the bait house and watched the wildly success-ful fishermen come off the pier and head to the parking lot, I wanted to go out on the pier so badly that I started to ache, down below my stomach, just above my left hip and toward the back. But I knew my parents were serious about their chorus, and I had no idea where I could find an adult who would be willing to walk me out on the pier and help me catch my own bucketful of perch.

The problem for me was that this week was a regular vaca-tion for my mom and me and my two little brothers, Bobby and Bruce, but only a partial vacation for my dad. Each year he wanted to save his week of vacation to take us somewhere up north, and yet he didn't want to keep my mom from missing the week when her side of the family camped together at Grand Haven. So he got up before sunrise — it was hard for him to be quiet with the frying pan as he made himself some eggs — then drove into Grand Rapids to the tool and die shop, and finally re-turned to the beach at night. It was exciting for me to walk Bobby and Bruce out to the main gate of the park just before supper, strain to spot our green Plymouth coming around the bend to the north, and then climb in with Dad as he wound from the gate to Diaper Alley. If his pants weren't too greasy, he would let one or the other of us sit on his lap and hold the steering wheel with him.

Still, he was gone all day, and he was always so tired at night that what he mainly wanted to do was sit around the campfire and hear what everyone had done during the day. "Remember," he'd tell me, "someone's got to be paying while all the rest of you are playing. Besides, you know that when you're older you'll have all the chances you could ever want to fish on the pier. You'll just have to bide your time."

I also didn't dare ask my mom to take me out on the pier. She probably would have had to take Bobby and Bruce along, and trying to keep the two of them from stepping on other people's fishing equipment or tripping off the pier would have been a challenge for a small cadre of highly trained and experienced child-care attendants. And at that point of my life, I didn't think she knew too much about fishing.

So I had a simple choice: I could work to develop a level of patience that I thought was unheard of among six-year-olds and wait a year or two until my parents said I could go out on the pier by myself, or I could mope around the campsite and try to project an aura of misery to everyone else. I chose to mope.

After a solid afternoon of some highly nuanced moping, I was surprised by my Uncle Arie. He had noticed that I wasn't hanging around with my cousins, and instead of bringing his concern to my mom, a response I was hoping for, he asked me directly what was going on.

"Aw, nothin', nothin' that anybody in this family needs to care about," I muttered as I made a slouching turn away from him.

But my mom overheard and cut in: "Billy? He's six years old but he's acting like the biggest baby on the alley, kicking out about things nobody can do a single thing about. So far this week he's been spending a bunch of time hanging around the bait house and watching people come off the pier loaded down with perch. We know he would love to go out on that pier. But we don't think he's old enough to head out there and fish by himself yet, and instead of accepting that and dealing with it, he's going to wreck a good part of the week for himself — and maybe for some of the rest of us, too."

Then Uncle Arie, I thought, started playing a cruel little game: "He wants to fish? Someone should have said something. I love catching Lake Michigan perch. And I've got all my gear stored under the trailer. We could have our own fish fry. Maybe a couple of them. I haven't gone out on the pier myself this week since Nancie and Joanie are so young and I didn't want to be a party pooper for anything here — besides, I like relaxing around the campsite, too. But if Bill wants to go, I can take him. We can go already tomorrow. If we get up early and get out there before the sun shows over the dunes, we should be able to catch a mess, clean them up, and be back here in time for breakfast."

"There, Billy, so what do you think now?" my mom asked.

"I think Uncle Arie should learn to tell the truth."

"Whoa, whoa, whoa. No need for a big smart mouth on a skinny little guy. That's my baby sister you're talking to, you know. I am telling the truth. I'll take you out tomorrow, and I'll bring all the gear; you just have to haul your little backside out of your sleeping bag a little after five. You really up for this?"

"Yeah! Absolutely. Sorry. I'll be ready. I'll ask my dad to wake me up when he gets up. This is unbelievable! I had no clue you knew how to fish."

I think I got a little sleep that night, but it wasn't very deep, and it didn't come until I had nearly twisted my sleeping bag into a knot around my neck. Two windows of thought kept opening up brightly in my mind, inviting me to move closer and examine the views.

One window opened on the pier. It got me wondering

about the fishing I would do the next day — whether the lake side or the channel side would be more productive, how deep in the water the perch were likely to be, whether we'd use bobbers or not, how long the fights would be, how hard it would be to unhook the fish, what the anglers around me would say when they saw the big fish I was catching, how heavy the perch would be to carry off the pier, and how Bobby and Bruce would look when they saw my catch.

The other opened on an image of Uncle Arie gazing across a stretch of turbulent water. I couldn't figure him out. He was just an uncle, a pretty good guy once I stopped to think about it, I guess, but he'd really never paid anything like special attention to my brothers and me, and I didn't know him well. "How tall you up to now, Billy boy?" he would ask when our families got together. "Tall enough to jump and touch the panels on the basement ceiling," I would brag. Then he would turn to Bobby and ask him when he was going to grow and catch up with me. He didn't bother with Bruce since he was so young and didn't do much except find creative ways to hurt himself.

When my mom's side of the family camped at the beach, about the only time my brothers and I really saw much of Uncle Arie was when we played our young-boy version of home-run derby with a whiffleball and a plastic bat, a game we tried to organize each day after supper. Bobby and I would round up our male cousins and as many other boys from Diaper Alley as we could. Then we would scoop out a shallow area to mark home plate, set out a small board with no nails in it for a pitcher's rubber, and stick cottonwood leaves in an arc in the sand to mark the home-run line. Finally we would pick sides (they varied only in the last couple of picks, who weren't really good enough to make much difference to the game) and get straight about the rules: any swing or foul or hit not over the home-run line was an out, each team had six outs per inning, and everyone on one team except the pitcher was allowed to stand just in front of the home-run line and jump to try to catch hits headed over the line, but they couldn't throw mitts or t-shirts or sand to try to knock the ball down. Once we started to play, Uncle Arie often would carry little Joanie over and sit on a picnic table with her to watch a few innings.

As I remember them, those games were remarkable not for any displays of athletic prowess, but for frequent and heated arguments about the effects of the swirling breezes along the lakeshore. Sometimes, for instance, one of the smaller kids on the other team would pop a ball into not-too-deep left field, and then a gust of wind would come up off the lake and carry the ball over all our heads and past the home-run line. The kid would look astonished, since he had never come close to a home run before, but a first home run was a first home run, and he took it.

"No fair," I would yell. "That's gotta count as the last out. No way that bloopy little pop-up was going over. Without the wind it wouldn't have come close. You can't accept that. It's an out or a do-over, one or the other."

Other times I would rip a shot deep into center field, start to exult with my teammates about how badly we were stomping the barbarians, and then watch in dismay as a gust would meet the ball head on, force it higher and higher, and then ever so gently push it back, back to my side of the home-run line, where it would eventually fall as one of our team's six outs.

"You got to be kidding me!" My voice went falsetto. "That

was a blast. It should have been a homer. Easily! It looked like it was gonna be the longest homer ever. It was all the wind. The wind held it up. That's about as fair as a gull crappin' on your head. It's a homer or a do-over, one or the other."

I lost every one of these arguments, mainly since the guys on the other team always said they would quit before going along with me. And at the end of one game, Uncle Arie had a response for me, too. As I was walking over to pick up the pitcher's rubber to store for next time, he carried Joanie over to me and asked, "Why all the bickering and squawking? If you're gonna play home-run derby out here, you're gonna have to get used to those gusts, even if they work against you sometimes. You can't control wind off the big lake. If you think you can, you haven't learned the first thing about control. It's a great game, with some wild and crazy twists. Why not accept it for what it is?"

Already at six I was learning how to talk big: "Giving in is for sissies," I said as I knocked the sand off the pitcher's rubber.

As I thought about perch and asked myself questions about Uncle Arie as I tried to get to sleep that night before fishing, it's no wonder that when I finally relaxed into some half-awake dreams I was almost startled by the images my mind juggled: giant perch with well trimmed orange mustaches jumping out of the water near my line and using ragged fins to fly onto the catwalk running down the middle of the pier, as well as my Uncle Arie dressed in a black robe and seated in something like a barber's chair, twirling a handkerchief and quizzing me about proper conduct on a big-league baseball field.

Once I got outside the next morning, though, I found Uncle Arie sitting on our picnic table in cut-offs and a sweatshirt, watching the taillights of cars headed out of the park toward Grand Haven and then Spring Lake. He had all our gear laid out neatly on the picnic table. He had two long bamboo poles, maybe nine feet long, with the line wrapped around the tips. He had a tool box that held hooks, lures, pliers, and spools of extra line. He had two folding stools. He had two buckets, one for our bait, the other for our catch. And he had a big life jacket for himself and a smaller one for me.

"How many minnows do you think we'll need?" he asked as we came up to the bait house.

"Oh, probably six or seven, two or three for me and two or three for you. Plus an extra one just to be safe."

"Six or seven? Are we gonna get into some fish or just monkey around? I think we'll need at least five dozen minnows. Sometimes you can use a minnow for more than one fish, but often they swallow it or spit it. And sometimes the minnows get so torn up they won't even stay on a hook. We're gonna catch a bucket-load of fish, so we'll need a bucket-load of minnows. While I'm paying for the minnows, why don't you carry the rest of our stuff out to those tables by the walkway?"

When he joined me with the minnows, for the first time in my life I actually marched to the end of the walkway and stepped onto the pier. For the first minute or so on the pier, I counted my steps.

"The farther out we can get, the better," he said, and we did manage to get out a little past the lighthouse near the halfway point before there was no room left. I wondered how early those who had made it all the way out to the house on the end had had to get up. Uncle Arie said that sometimes people showed up at dusk and stayed out there all night and well into the next day.

When he rigged up my pole, Uncle Arie surprised me. At the very end of my line he attached a sinker. Then a foot above the sinker he used a special knot to tie on a hook. Then a foot above that first hook he tied on a second one.

"Two hooks? You fish with two hooks?"

"This is the real deal, Billy. I told you we're gonna catch some fish, and I wasn't just blowing hot air around. You didn't think all those guys carrying fifty or a hundred fish off the pier catch them all one at a time, did you?"

I hadn't known enough to think anything else, but I didn't admit it. Then Uncle Arie showed me how to hook up a minnow — just through the lips, not so deeply that the hook goes through the brain, but not so lightly that the minnow can pull itself free. He did one for me, and then I tried to hook up another. With the minnow squirming wildly in my hands, leaving tiny silver flecks on my fingers, and with my hands shaking a little with all the anticipation, it took me a while before I had two minnows dangling from the hooks.

"Lower your line until the sinker hits the bottom, no more than that. You've got to keep the minnows just off the bottom. Then take up the slack. You've got to keep a tight line to feel the bites," Uncle Arie told me.

I wondered how long it would take for me to get a bite. "Please, God, please, don't let me be the only one who doesn't catch anything out here," I prayed under my breath. I had already seen lots of people pulling perch in. And then I felt a sequence of insistent little taps on my line and then nothing at all. What was that? I wondered. It felt like something had done a little strumming on my line. Then I felt a sharp jerk, and I watched my line cut sidewise along the surface. I clamped the butt of the pole to my side with my right elbow, put my left hand above my right as far out on the pole as I could reach, pulled up hard, and hauled out of the water a perch that looked to be over a foot long, its body in a tight shimmy of resistance to my hook. All I had to do then was swing the fish back toward my uncle and me, but I brought the fish back too hard, and it swung past both of us and then up again, at the peak of its backward arc almost smacking an older boy on the cheek as he walked down the middle of the pier.

"A little more gently next time, OK Billy?" Uncle Arie whispered. "Trapeze it back just fast enough so that we can catch it. Just get it started, and it'll come in to us."

It took me only a fish or two to learn. And for the next sixty minutes, sitting with my legs hanging over the edge of the pier, I had more fun than I had ever had before in an hour in the six years and some days I had lived to that point. Four different times I caught two fish at once. Put a couple more hooks on my line, I thought, and I might not be able to lift all the fish that bite. When Uncle Arie wasn't helping me unhook fish, he was going just as fast as I was. The two of us laughed, made up dumb little chants that were supposed to keep the fish in the mood, and punched each other on the shoulder. Once he even leaned back, laid his head on the cement behind him, and closed his eyes for a few seconds.

By the time we headed in for breakfast, we had caught forty-seven perch. I wanted to carry the bucket of perch in by myself, but Uncle Arie had to help me. Even with two of us sharing the weight, the handle cut sharply into my hands. As we carried the bucket off the pier, I kept reminding myself that this was no dream, that I was going to get older and bigger in a world where it was possible for two people to catch almost fifty perch in less than an hour. I thought of it as a world at first light.

Much later that day, after the moms had fried all those perch up for the extended family to enjoy, my mom asked Uncle Arie whether the two of us had talked about making another trip to the pier the next day.

"No, we were so busy hooking up minnows and unhooking perch that we didn't even think about tomorrow. I'm willing to try again. We can go if Billy wants to. It's just that I listened to the six o'clock news, and I guess we're due for a pretty dramatic change in the weather. A front's clipping in tonight, and after it goes through the wind will probably shift around to the east. East winds blow all the warmer surface water out into the lake, letting cold water from below come up and in; and from what I've seen in the past, the perch stop biting. Maybe they're too cold to bite. Or maybe they follow the warmer water out. Anyway, it's up to Billy. I like being out there whether the fish are biting or not; I like watching the boats in the channel. We might be able to catch a couple of perch. Then again, we might sit out there all morning and get skunked. So what do you think, bud?"

"You mean we can go out there one day and not have enough hands and then go again the next day and not get a bite?"

"That's the way it is."

"Well, that's not the way it should be. I guess I'd just as soon wait till it's good again."

But for the rest of our week at the beach, the wind stayed strong from the east. So that was the only time Uncle Arie and I went out together on the pier to fish. And in the nearly fifty years since then, we never fished together again, on the pier at Grand Haven or anywhere else. I don't know exactly why. Maybe it was because Uncle Arie started to like golf more and more and couldn't find time for fishing. Maybe it was because of a change in the lake: at some point after that special week, alewives swarmed into Lake Michigan while the perch seemed to disappear. I just can't say for sure.

What I can say is that in the years since we teamed up to catch all those perch, Uncle Arie and I have been around each other quite frequently: at reunions at Long Lake Park in the summer, during Thanksgiving meals with the extended family spread out around one big table and three or four card tables, and on Christmas Eves at Grandma Fannie's. But that time on the pier with him back when I was six was clearly the sweetest time we ever shared.

Not long after Uncle Arie retired from his job with the power company, he started his noticeable decline, not with one catastrophic event but with a series of small strokes. He had his first while he was in his backyard raking up some leaves. He told us afterwards that he had felt dizzy, somewhat short of breath, and he wasn't sure where he was, a little like waking up in a strange room and not knowing where the door is. Aunt Hattie found him on his hands and knees in a small pile of birch leaves, rummaging around as if looking for coins.

His doctor said that there was nothing like a cure for Uncle Arie. He put him on some blood-thinning medication (really risky stuff, a few in the family said) and emphasized that he should keep doing everything that he had already been working on in order to try to control his blood pressure — go light on the salt, walk at least three times a week, lose some weight, not let the small stuff get to him.

But a few weeks later Uncle Arie had another episode. After three of these, or perhaps more that no one knew of, he really started to slide. He always seemed tired. Even in places that should have been familiar to him, he acted as if he were deeply disoriented, on the edge of panic. Much of the right side of his body was paralyzed, even parts of his face. His right cheek and the right side of his mouth and jaw were frozen in an expression that some people saw as a grin, others as a grimace. And from the right corner of his mouth he would drool if left unattended, the saliva running down his chin and dripping into expanding patterns on his shirt.

After his first stroke, he was still able to get quite a few recognizable words out, but he did so only with an enormous and obviously frustrating physical effort. A couple of simple statements could almost exhaust him. After the third stroke, he acted as if he understood what those around him were saying, and he often made gurgling little moans in response, but he never again said a word that anyone else could figure out.

For a while, everyone in the family urged Aunt Hattie to get some help, to hire a nurse to stop by each day for a few hours or to sell the house and move into assisted living. "The Holland Home really knows how to take care of stroke victims, and they've been advertising on the radio a lot lately — maybe they've got some good deals," everyone repeated.

"I'm still strong in lots of ways," Aunt Hattie always responded. "Plus I love this old house. And the neighborhood.

Where would my neighbors and I be without one another? We've been together longer than many people get to live. What if they need to borrow some vanilla? We'll stay here. I'll take care of Arie. I've taken care of someone or other practically my whole life. No one's asking me to do something I don't know how to do."

And so they stayed in their red-brick Cape Cod with the pots of geraniums on the edges of the front porch. Aunt Hattie didn't get out as much as she had in the past, but she told everyone she was fine. Uncle Arie had always loved being outside, and somehow he communicated to Aunt Hattie that when the weather was mild she should open the door of the garage, wheel him to within a foot or two of the opening — so he wouldn't get wet if it started to rain — and let him sit there and watch for passing traffic while strapped in his chair, leaving all those on the street to try to figure out from a distance what his expression meant.

As I grew older, I wondered what, if anything, I could do when people have strokes or get liver cancer or start having tremors. The fact is that most of us don't have much time to invest. Or we really don't know what we should do to help. But whenever I thought of my Uncle Arie sitting in his garage waiting for some car or truck to drive by, I knew I had to do something to bring some spice back into his life. I mean, his sitting there was pathetic. They lived on a cul de sac, of all places, and he usually saw no more than a vehicle or two per hour — on a busy day. Imagine if some UPS truck coming down the street were the highlight of your morning.

So I came up with a plan and proposed it to my Aunt Hattie.

"What if," I asked, "what if every couple of weeks in the

summer I take an afternoon off and pick up Uncle Arie for a ride? We could drive out by the airport, or I could show him the parts of the South Beltline that are finished. Give me a week or two, and I'll think of some other places. Has he seen where they have 'blues on the mall' downtown? Don't you think it would be good for him to get out a little?"

"I'm sure he would like that, Bill. But he's going to need more than a little help. On this end I can help get him in the car and — "

"What do you mean — I'm gonna have to help him with the bathroom or something?"

"No, I'll take care of all that — I'll have him in a fresh Depends. But he hates it when he drools on his shirt. And sometimes in the car he slumps over to one side and needs help staying up straight. You'd probably have to use a pillow or something to wedge against the door to prop him up. Most of all, though, he really seems to dislike having to get out of the car in places that he thinks are unfamiliar — and he thinks just about everywhere except our house and the garage is unfamiliar now. He can look out the windows, but don't take him out and wheel him around. For some reason it's way too frightening — he acts real panicky."

"Well, those aren't the world's biggest challenges. I can wipe off his chin with a hanky. Plus we've got some old foam pads in the garage that I can use to help keep him up straight in the seat. And we don't have to get out of the car at all. We can just drive and look. Maybe I'll find places where I can park and point out stuff for him. How does next Tuesday sound?"

"All right. All right. Next Tuesday should work, if you really want to try. I've actually been hoping for a chance to get my hair cut."

Even as we talked, I had a destination in mind, and it wasn't the airport or the South Beltline or downtown Grand Rapids. When I returned the next week, as Aunt Hattie helped me move Uncle Arie from his chair into the front seat of our van, she asked me where I was planning to go.

"It's an afternoon mystery tour," I laughed. "All I'm gonna say right now is that we're headed west and that we'll be back by five. You just enjoy the haircut. We'll enjoy the excursion."

I headed out Leonard Street, taking one of the slower and more scenic routes to Grand Haven. Initially I had thought it would be great to wheel him on the walkway along the channel and right out onto the south pier, stopping for a few minutes near our special spot of about fifty years ago. But my aunt's words about his discomfort when he was out of the car in unfamiliar places gave me a different idea.

As I was leaving Spring Lake, instead of curving off south and going over the drawbridge to Grand Haven, I took the ramp to Fruitport, drove by a small strip mall, through some dunes, and past cottages with signs carrying punning names (a retired algebra teacher, I had been told, lived in the place called "Aftermath"). As I approached the channel, I turned right and parked in the public lot almost directly across the channel from where the bait house had once stood.

"There," I said as I pointed across to our spot on the pier. No one was there. In fact, no one was anywhere on the pier. The wind that afternoon was strong from the southwest, and waves were breaking over the pier all along its course. Anyone walking out there could easily have been swept into the channel. I pointed again. "There," I repeated, and left my arm extended for a few seconds.

Uncle Arie turned his wobbly head and gazed across the water. I studied his expression. I was hoping for a glint in his eyes, some sign that he recalled our joy that day and that somewhere inside he retained some of the energy, skill, and competence that had set that joy up. If he was able to recognize our spot, maybe it would be worth bringing him out here again.

Did he recognize it? I can't say. He gazed, never changed his expression, and, although his Adam's apple bobbed, he made no sound. I noticed that a line of moisture ran down his chin. I pulled out my handkerchief and wiped it off, as gently as I could. Then I started the car, pulled out of the parking lot, drove back through Spring Lake, and took the freeway home.

After bringing him home and telling Aunt Hattie where we had gone, I said that I'd call in the next day or so to check on his reaction to the trip.

"Tell me," I asked the following day, "was Uncle Arie any different after the drive? Did it bring anything back? Did it set off a spark or two?"

"Hard to say. When I asked him last night about the afternoon, he didn't make much noise. And now he's outside again in his chair waiting for some traffic. The postman usually drives by right about now. If there's any difference, it's maybe in his sleep. Last night he didn't seem quite as restless as he usually is when we go to bed. Most nights he just can't seem to find any peace. But last night there was a little more stillness in him."

"Well, that's a small mercy, I guess."

"At this age, I never sort mercies out into different sizes."

"Aunt Hattie, how do you do it? I mean, these are supposed to be some of your best years, when you're finally able to do everything you've put off for so long. How do you keep it in? Most days, aren't you about ready to scream?"

"I have my times, believe you me. I have my times. But I remind myself of what Arie said, back after his very first stroke, when he could still talk. Lots of people who had worked with Arie used to stop by back then, and one of them once asked Arie if he felt the stroke had cheated him. The man didn't put it exactly that way, but I won't use the language he used."

"I've never heard this story. What did Uncle Arie say?"

"He said, 'I'm not the one who knows the path of the wind.' That visitor didn't have a clue what Arie meant, and he dropped the subject. I think he figured Arie was talking nonsense."

"'The one who knows the path of the wind'? I'm not sure I get it either."

"Well, I didn't right away. But then I did some checking, and now I probably wouldn't get through a single day without reminding myself of what Arie meant." ◐

The Soul's Sincere Desire?

I have a question about prayer. More to the point, I have a question about a specific possible prayer by a specific actual person — me.

This question has been festering near the edges of my consciousness for at least ten years now. It first formed when one of my colleagues, reacting to a manuscript she was reviewing, a manuscript about meditation, asked whether I thought it was ever proper to use the word *please* in prayers.

She thought it was unnecessary. God knows, she argued, exactly what we want and what we need, and for us to do something like plead or implore with a "please, Lord" this and a "please, Lord" that was to fall into the tight circle of redundancy. And, she concluded, who has time for redundancy?

But I was less sure. When I reviewed my own prayers, I couldn't recall whether I had ever used a "please" or not. And to add a "please" or two to a new prayer seemed very much like an experiment, one raising disturbing questions about variables I probably couldn't control.

Such thoughts led directly to the question that has been vexing me: Would it ever be acceptable in God's eyes for me to pray for success, maybe even marked success, in fishing?

Part of me suspected that it could never be acceptable. After all, I reasoned, fishing probably isn't the most important thing in life, and maybe I should take care not to ask God about less than really important things. What if a serious matter of health or safety confronted my family or me and by then God had come to regard me as someone who was continually bringing only relatively trivial things before him? Was it even possible that, by the time a crisis came along, I could have reached some kind of personal limit for petitions granted?

At the same time, I knew perfectly well that sometimes the conditions on the days when I went fishing were not very promising. On a Sunday I might plan to go fishing the following Thursday, and when that Thursday arrived, all indications would point to a tough day for fishing. Not too long ago, for instance, a strong wind was blowing off the marshes on the east side of Muskegon Lake on the day Duzzer, my fishing partner, and I had decided to fish there. The wind by itself made controlling the boat difficult, but the fact that it was from the east was a sign that atmospheric conditions were poor for fishing. One of the first sayings I learned and trusted as a boy was that "When the wind is in the east, that's when the fishees bite the least!"

On such a day, was it appropriate to ask God to bless me with a limit of bass, and maybe even big bass at that? How much respect and reverence would I be showing by asking for something that common fishing sense indicated was highly unlikely if not close to impossible? I might just as well ask for a miracle almost two millennia after the time Christ gave his disciples a startling lesson about where to cast their nets.

So maybe praying for a blessing on my fishing was not right.

But there are some things about Duzzer that bring prayers to my mind.

To be fair to him, I should note that we have been fishing together for over thirty-five years now and that in almost all ways we make an excellent team. Each of us likes to fish for the same kinds of fish. Thus we never have the kinds of disputes that break out when one person likes to sit and wait for catfish to inhale gobs of crawlers while another likes to troll with artificial minnows for walleye. And we know how much to talk while in the boat; we sense when silence has stretched on a little too long, but we never cross the line into distracting jabber. Finally, we have similar amounts of patience and stamina. We have found that by stocking a Coleman cooler with submarine sandwiches and Power Aid and by putting a large coffee can to creative and furtive use, we are able to stay in the boat for really long periods of time, once as long as twelve hours straight.

But Duzzer has a frustrating habit or two. For one thing, he keeps track of how many fish each of us catches. He never does this out loud, with detailed updates about the day's fishing activity and times to gloat. In his tackle box he keeps two small plastic counters — one blue and one pink — that he found at a dollar store and that were intended, I think, to help husband-and-wife golfers keep track of their strokes. Duzzer uses the blue one to record each of the fish that he catches and the pink one to record some of the fish that I catch.

When he catches a fish, he never says a thing about these counters. He holds up and admires the fish from several angles, overestimates how long it is, gives it a little kiss on the mouth, releases it, leans over the edge of the boat to wash off his hands, carefully dries his hands on a ragged towel, and then reaches into his tackle box and adds a number to his counter with a tell-tale little click. Throughout it all, he looks as if he can think of no way to grow more satisfied with himself.

When I catch a fish, he again never says a thing about these counters. I might go through almost the same process as he does: holding up and admiring the fish, giving an estimate of how long it is, pretending to buss it, releasing it, washing off and drying my hands. Then I listen carefully to hear whether he thinks my fish is worthy to be added to my clicker or not. If he thinks it's not big enough, he never reaches into his tackle box; he just keeps on casting.

So at the end of the day the numbers on the clickers don't necessarily reflect our respective success. As we come back to the launch site, people on other boats and on docks invariably call out, asking "how'd you do today?" or "catch anything?" or "how they been biting?" If the number on his clicker is higher than the one on mine, he usually says something like, "Yeah. A good day. I got quite a few — several big ones."

What irks me even more occurs on days when I have caught many more and many larger fish than he has. In response to queries on such days, he usually says something like, "Pretty slow today. We caught a few, but overall we had to work like fools for what we caught, and the ones we got were kinda runty."

Thus I am often sorely tempted to pray, "Lord, grant that I might have an amazing day in the boat today. If somehow you don't want to work it out for me to catch dozens and dozens of fish, then, Lord, help me to catch something really big, maybe close to a state record, something so impressive that we'll have to take it to a bait shop to have it weighed and photographed. And Lord, make it so that the picture and a story accompanying it appear in the local newspapers. When I'm interviewed, I will try to remember to mention that Duzzer helped out by netting the fish."

Some weeks ago I was getting to the point where I couldn't tell whether I was just considering and rehearsing these words or actually praying them. So I thought I'd better get some professional advice about the acceptability of such a prayer. I decided to call a friend of mine who had gone to seminary. I had gotten to know him quite well when we both worked in a furniture factory after college, during which time he decided it was his calling to make disciples, not dowels. So I called him up, and we set a date to meet for what we often ate during those earlier lunch hours away from sawdust — liver and onions.

Throughout lunch, he listened supportively (he had taken a half-day workshop in listening, he told me) as I explained what I was thinking of asking God and why.

After I finished, he was silent for a bit, and then he asked, "In all of this, have you thought hard and well about what you're seeking?"

"Seeking? I don't have to think hard about that — I'm looking for an answer, a clear answer."

"No, no, what are you seeking?"

"Oh, OK, I get it now — a really impressive fish, a news flash of a fish. A fish that will get me in the record books even."

"No, no, listen: What are you seeking first of all?"

That did it. If he wanted to betray our friendship and frustrate me playing twenty questions, especially when I was struggling with such a serious theological question, then I didn't have the time. I had to get back to work. I looked up, caught the waiter's eye, and said, "Check!" ✆

Frogs

When I watched each of my three sons take his turn flailing the nursery air after birth, my first clear thought was that we had some serious work to do to smooth out those jerky arm motions before they could become the fine fly fishermen I hoped they would be.

Only a few years after the third one was born, therefore, I bought three pairs of rubber boots, which looked like hip boots on the boys. I decided to start them out with casting gear, and I searched until I found some nearly unbreakable fiberglass rods and dependable reels.

I also talked to several people about where we should fish, eventually deciding on Myers Lake, about twenty minutes northeast of Grand Rapids. Once you step off its banks into the water, you rarely sink very far into the mud, never far enough to risk losing boots or to make young boys think they're being sucked into a hole. And in late May and early June, bluegills and sunfish aggressively bite on most anything tossed near their spawning beds in the shallow water.

When we set out, the boys were still pretty young — Jon was seven, Joel was six, and Jason was three. But I thought that the sooner they started, the sooner they could overcome the frustrations of learning and develop true skill.

Once we reached the lake, the boys obeyed without a squawk when I told them to sit on a picnic table while I finished rigging their poles. But as we walked to the shore, a leopard frog jumped across Jason's path.

And that was the first of dozens, all basking in the sun near the shore till we came trundling through. Then they went into a popcorn frenzy of jumping — many into the water, many past us to the rear, a few actually bouncing off our legs.

The boys took several quick looks — at me, at one another, and at the frogs. Then, simultaneously, they dropped their rods, yanked off their boots and socks, and started creeping and lunging after the frogs. Soon they persuaded me, starting to sweat in my waders, to get down on hands and knees and try to herd the frogs toward the flexing traps of their fleshy little hands.

When one would catch a frog, he would bring it over to show it off. "Look, Dad, look!" he exulted as the nearly squished frog excreted orangish liquid through his fingers and down his forearm. "It's a great big one, maybe the king of all the frogs, but leaking like crazy!"

They were not happy when after forty minutes or so I marched them back to the car, grass stains on their shorts, the greenish residue of goose droppings on their knees, blades of grass between their toes.

"But I thought we came here to fish," Jon complained.

"I thought so, too. But we sure can't fish now. When you guys tossed your rods on the ground, you weren't thinking very well about what you were doing. You got the lines all tangled up, and there's sand in the reels — if we use them now, we'll wreck the gears."

They sulked for a while, but on the way home it took them only a couple of miles before they started arguing about who had caught the most frogs, the largest frog, the fastest frog, the rarest frog, the most colorful frog, the frog with the biggest potential croak, and on and on.

"How did it go? Aren't you home a little early?" Wanda asked as I carried the mass of rods into the basement.

"It was a mess," I sighed. "We never even once got a line in the water. We walked into jumping frogs near the shore, and all the boys wanted to do was chase them."

"It was bad? When the boys came in, they were really excited, chattering away like crazy — I was sure they'd had a great time."

"The boys? Why doesn't anyone in this world ever think about me? It was chaos. And now I have half a day's work trying to untangle the lines and clean out the reels. No plan should get as messed up as that one did. I'm going to have to learn to control these little excursions a lot better in the future. I don't think I'll dare take all three of them fishing at the same time ever again. Just imagine — chasing frogs when they could have been catching fish."

After that, I usually took one at a time fishing. And I guided each one through a precise sequence of stages: Each first learned to use casting equipment, then spinning equipment, and finally fly-fishing equipment. Each in his turn made impressive progress, and I took silent but ample pride in their development.

About a dozen years after the fiasco at Myers Lake, Jason and

I were resting on a bank of the Au Sable River at dusk, waiting for the wonder of the hex hatch to start. The crickets and peepers seemed intent on crushing us with their clamor, and every thirty seconds or so a bullfrog would belch out such an alarming croak that we would jump a little and then move a bit closer to each other.

"That last one must be the king of all the bullfrogs," Jason whispered.

"I guess."

"Dad?"

"Yeah?"

"Do you remember that day when I was super little and you took us out to that beach to hunt frogs?"

"Huh?"

"That time all three of us guys had such a blast catching those frogs together? And you were crawling around with us. You were so excited, I remember, that you never even took off your waders. You weren't the best frog-catcher, though. And all the time you had goose crap smeared on your cheek. That was a mad-awesome day. Do you remember it?"

"Hmmm."

"Do you?"

"I'm afraid it's coming back to me." ⑥

Wilderness Survival Kit

"Why this sudden spike of fear?" I asked myself.

True, I was easing the van around several deep ruts at the same time that I was trying to avoid a pine branch hanging in aggrieved splinters over the narrow road leading west toward Waugoshance Point in Wilderness State Park. But, I insisted to myself, you've spent hours jouncing along logging roads in northern Ontario, miles from any source of help. And only a mile or so back you passed a general store set amid several cottages and before that a sprawling campground filled with RVs and tents.

In part, I finally decided, it was the sudden dark wildness that I was reacting to, wildness that had been kept out beyond the shoulders of the road until the blacktop of Wilderness Park Drive narrowed and gave way to the dirt and gravel of Waugoshance Point Road. Then the wildness was all around.

Also, I thought, I was probably reacting to the fact that I was not alone. Jon, our oldest, was lying in what our family called the "way-back" of the van, rhythmic in his narrow whistle of a snore despite being bounced around by the rough road. It was great having him along — here we were, a father-and-son team, ready to venture into some lightly explored waters that others would ask us about for years. Jon was resourceful and resilient. But he was just a kid, and he clearly was depending on me. If some kind of trouble were to come up, and if I had been on my own, I was sure that I could handle it. What hadn't I handled in the past, in all those years before children, when I took risks in the outdoors just to remind myself what adrenaline felt like? Now I was worried about what it would be like to face trouble with a terrified eight-year-old clinging to me, sobbing to be back home with Wanda and his brothers. I wasn't used to being in wild places with someone who couldn't take care of himself.

We had come to Wilderness because of a tantalizing description I had heard several years earlier.

"Smallmouth bass?" my friend Arnie had picked up on one of my comments. "You like to fish for smallmouth?"

"I love it! I love it about as much as I love peach slices and Wheaties for breakfast!"

"Well then, have you ever fished along the south shore of the peninsula leading out to Waugoshance Point up west of the bridge?"

"Isn't that in Wilderness State Park? I've heard of the park, something about remote cabins for rent, but I've never heard much about Waugoshance Point. What's so special about the water up there?"

"Special? It's a light-year beyond dreams, man! Drive as far as you can on Waugoshance Point Road, find the little parking area, pull the car up under a cedar tree for some shade, grab your rod and load whatever else you need in a rucksack, and then head off southwest toward the water. In the water you'll see boulders all over the place and rocky shoals that you can walk along way out into the bay — the shoals are usually just a foot or so under the surface of the water. You'll catch smallmouth around all those boulders and shoals, too, but it pays to be a little picky. Look for the biggest boulders you can find that are completely under the water. If a boulder's not under the water, gulls will sit on it, and if they do, fish will leave the neighborhood. Once you find the right boulders — and I'm talking about boulders the size of Volkswagens — cast right next to them and be prepared. I once caught a smallmouth on every last one of thirty-six consecutive casts. Every one of those fish was absent from school the day there were lessons on how to give up. And maybe the best thing of all is that no one will ever be around to try to horn in on your spot."

"Are you serious?"

"Do I fib? About fishing?"

About fishing he always told the truth, and I immediately started imagining a trip to Wilderness. But other fishing spots, spots closer to home, beckoned more insistently, and I thought that I should wait to try Wilderness until at least one of my sons could handle walking around on the slippery rocks of shoals.

When Jon was nearing the end of fourth grade (we had started him in school as early as possible), I made plans for us to spend a weekend casting for upper Lake Michigan smallmouth.

The spike of fear that I had experienced upon leaving the blacktop for the dirt was just that — only a spike. And I gradually stopped worrying about being stranded with a young boy and started enjoying the sights and scents of the drive. Along the way, we passed gates on two-tracks leading to the remote cabins — five of them, I think — and at the end of the road I found some cedars to nose the van under.

Then we did exactly what Arnie had recommended. At least

one of the boulders along the edge of the small parking area had a relatively flat top, and we used it to lay out and sort our gear. Then we packed all that gear up in pockets of a rucksack and started to pull on our waders. I got mine on easily and grabbed my rod, eager to head off to the distant shimmer of water.

But Jon was fussing. He had his waders pulled up almost to his waist, and he was working to adjust the strap on a little fanny pack that he apparently intended to wear under his waders.

"What's in there? You sure you want to have that along, especially under your waders? That might get pretty uncomfortable after a while."

"Sure I do. Don't you remember what this is? It's my wilderness survival kit. I got it after I was initiated into Cadets. My counselors said it holds everything a person needs to survive in the wilds. And here we are in Wilderness State Park. It's like the perfect place to try it out. It'll stay dry under my waders."

"I get what you're thinking. But I'm not sure you'll need it. I know exactly where we're heading — I'm tall enough to see the area from here. You really want to carry anything more than you absolutely have to?"

"Sure I do. Doesn't Grandpa always say you can never be too prepared?"

"Yeah, he does. So take it, but just hurry it up a little, OK?" With that I turned away and coughed off a snicker — it was all too cute. When I had been in Calvinist Cadets, they actually focused on skills needed in the outdoors. We hiked, camped, built rope bridges, and learned what wild plants were edible. But by the time Jon joined, they hardly ever left the church basement; they were always building rockets and crystal radio sets and

Pinewood Derby cars. What did they know about survival in the wilderness?

When Jon finally had all his gear on, we started off toward the water. But it took us longer than I expected to get there. For one thing, it wasn't the easiest walking we had ever done, making our way along a trail that in some places was muddy and in other places was hard and cobbled unevenly by fist-sized stones. For another thing, Jon periodically had to pause and adjust the position of his fanny pack — his waders were rubbing against it weird, he said.

But the going was slow mainly because there was so much to stop and inspect. Jon, who from the time he was a toddler never just walked but always walked and looked and saw, noticed most things first and pointed them out for me.

Snakes with delicate yellow stripes would startle us as they twined through the dry husks of pencil reeds. On the edges of little sloughs we would startle frogs, and they exploded away from us in repeating semicircles. In the sloughs we waded past some of the largest leeches either of us had ever seen; they couldn't suck through waders, we assured each other. When the sloughs grew into ponds, we found ourselves walking through a fish nursery, spotting a school of inch-long perch pivoting as one here, a cluster of shiners flashing there, and then a small pike lying almost hidden above a bed of moss. Off just on the edge of our vision was a great blue heron, one leg cocked in the air.

When we had started down the trail, we ran into a man and woman who were debating where to hike. They had hoped to walk out on the north shore of the peninsula, they told us, but it was roped off to allow piping plovers to breed. We left them as they pored over a map, and we never saw them again. Later we thought we saw a man fishing in a shallow bay, but as we got closer we noticed that he wasn't moving very much. Then we realized that what we were seeing was really a carefully balanced stack of flat rocks, some gull feathers protruding from cracks near its top.

Once we made it out of ponds to what could be considered part of Lake Michigan itself, we rigged up and started to fish.

I opted for a bronze Mepps spinner, largely because I could cover a lot of water in a short time with it. And it didn't hurt that it was close to the color of crayfish, I thought.

Jon used a reddish-brown tube jig. He couldn't cover water as fast as I, but he thought that he could more readily trigger the smallmouths by dragging the tube through sand and silt, stirring up little trails on the bottom.

And we did catch fish, one here and one there for a total of about two dozen for the day, usually along the edges of shoals or off the sides of big rocks in water that was deep enough to take on a greenish tint.

Pretty good fishing, I thought, but it was clearly not the fishing that Arnie had described. And since I had spent much of my earlier life worrying about whether my sons were catching fish fast enough to keep them interested, I had picked out another spot, a lake nearer Mackinac City, where we could wade and cast among reeds for pike on the second day of our trip if the first day turned out to be close to a dud.

"Well," I asked Jon on the hike back to our car, "what do you think? That wasn't the fastest fishing in the world, so we can go somewhere else tomorrow if you want. I know another place."

"I keep thinking about those huge boulders your friend

talked about. We have another day up north, right? Let's go farther down the coast and then try following shoals out deeper.
No way I want to go home and say we never even found what
we were looking for. Joel for sure and maybe even little Jason
will mock us to death."

"OK. But are you sure you're up to more serious exploration? From where we fished today we could see the line of trees
leading back to the parking lot. Tomorrow we're going to have
to really push it out away from here."

"If your old legs can maybe handle it, my young ones sure
can. Let's go for it."

So the next morning, we packed the same gear and then
took a longer hike west out the middle of the peninsula before
we veered to the southwest and started looking for good spots
to fish. It was so hazy as we left the parking lot that I couldn't
pinpoint the sun, but I was thankful not to have it shining directly on us as we walked up a sweat in waders. We tried to
make good time, but again Jon called me to stop and look — at
the blue, yellow, and white points of wildflowers; at what appeared to be a rusty old farm implement (farming in these
rocks and sand and shells?); and, finally, at a fragment of a
Petoskey stone resting among delicate bleached bones.

After forty-five minutes — probably more than two miles
— we veered off southwest. The moment I could see past the
sloughs and ponds, I became disoriented, almost dizzy. On the
bay I thought I saw dozens of floes, floes of old and somewhat
discolored ice, ice with gray marbling the white.

"Ice in summer in Michigan?" I was so surprised that I
didn't keep the words to myself.

"It looks a lot like ice, Dad," Jon said, "little icebergs, but it's not ice — it's fog, swirly little patches of fog. They're floating around all over the surface of the bay. We can still fish, can't we?"

"Sure — smallmouth might even like it if it's a little foggy out."

The territory we explored first was similar to that which we had fished the day before, with shoals extending in rust-colored lines and boulders scattered erratically. We decided to start by fishing our way out along a shoal that seemed to extend about halfway out to where waves were gently breaking. Jon worked along one edge; I worked along the other.

After a few minutes, I heard Jon's excited whisper, almost a hiss, carrying to me across the shoal: "Dad, get over here. You got to see this."

I eased my way across the shoal and saw what had gotten his attention. In a slot of emerald water off the edge of the shoal in front of him was a boulder the size of an elliptical conference table — ten people in wetsuits could have had a meeting around it. It had a remarkably flat top. It was entirely under the water. And when I looked even closer, I noticed that it was not in one section but two, one section pointing to shore, the other pointing out toward the bay. A foot-wide crack running parallel to the waves separated one section from the other.

"Watch this," he said; "I've got an idea." He checked his knot, tested his drag, and then flipped his tube right on top of the outer section. The remnants of waves weren't high, but they were strong enough to wash his tube shoreward and then over the edge and down into the crack.

"Fish on!" he gurgled. "Many people look for fish; Jon finds!"

After the fight, he waited for me to cast. I switched over to a tube. Then I flipped it onto the outermost chunk and waited for the waves to wash it into the crack. When they did, I took up the slack in my line, immediately felt the fish's take, and then tried to keep a smallmouth with muscles toned in cold water from pulling me off the rock I was balanced on. After I finally landed the fish, it was Jon's turn again.

I'd like to be able to report precisely how many fish we caught and released in that spot, but we were so busy reeling and unhooking fish and throwing our heads back and laughing for the unrestrained joy of it all that we lost track.

After twenty minutes the fishing slowed, and we decided to follow the shoal out into even deeper water. The patches of fog were putting on a little bulk, I thought. Still, we had no trouble finding another boulder in water of the same deep color. It was probably bigger than the first boulder, with more jagged edges, but it wasn't cracked. We threw into the shade along its side and started laughing all over again.

"This is the kind of fishing your friend was talking about," Jon exulted. "And people say Lewis and Clark were good at finding stuff!"

"Yeah, and it took us only a day and a half!"

"You don't have to tell me! Wait a minute! Look. Dad, do you think we could use that little gravel bar to wade across to that shoal over there? It goes out even farther than the one we're on. Maybe as the water around it gets deeper and deeper, we'll find more of these monster boulders."

"Let's try. It looks easy enough to cross."

We both used the bar to jump shoals, and then we started to follow the dull red of our new shoal deeper into the bay. After a hundred yards of rather slippery going, Jon noticed off to our right a sunken island that looked about as big as a little-league field.

"Look, Dad, look over there — it's huge, all gravel and busted-up shells and stuff, and only a foot or so under the water. I bet it's got a lot of those boulders we're looking for off its edge."

"Maybe you're right about the boulders, but look at the color of the water we'd have to get through. That's the darkest green we've seen so far — that water's got to be deep. I might be able to wade through it without getting water over my waders, but I bet you can't. We'd probably better not risk it."

"Wait — it looks way too good to pass up. How about a piggyback ride? Who's going to see us way out here if I ride your back in waders? I'm not too old for a ride. And the bottom is mostly sandy, it looks like."

"OK, maybe a cautious try. Hop on. You take both rods and don't let the reels dangle in the water. Maybe I can get us over there."

Jon rode my back as he did as a toddler, practically choking me with an arm around my neck, using his legs to try to shinny up my sides. The water never got deep enough to come over my waders, and I soon turned around and leaned back slightly to set him down on the edge of the island.

"I'll go out along the side toward the bay. You take the side toward shore," I told him. "Whoever finds a good boulder first calls for the other. A plan?"

"A plan."

We separated, and I moved off carefully along the edge, thinking I saw the dark and indistinct shape of a boulder in water off the island twenty or twenty-five yards ahead of me.

When I got closer, I realized with a little pulse of pride that it was an enormous boulder, and I started debating where I should cast first — I thought I'd test the boulder out first and then call for Jon if it held fish. I also decided to bite off about a foot of my line and tie a new knot: The boulder lay in the deepest water I had seen so far, and if I was ever going to tie into something like a record smallmouth up here, this could well be the place.

My first knot didn't hold; I must have missed a loop. When I finally tied a good knot and looked up, a jolt seared its way from my shoulder blades up through the back of my neck. How could that happen? Where did the boulder go? No, no, it was probably still right out there in front of me — it was just that while I had had my head down, several patches of fog had coalesced into a thick little cloud and had begun churning slowly on the water between me and where I was sure the boulder was.

"Just hold on a second," I told myself; "it's got to lift."

But it grew from the inside, billowing out to the sides and sending shape-shifting tentacles toward and then past me. I wheeled and looked for Jon. He had already been enfolded from other directions.

"Jon!" I screamed. "The fog closed in all at once. We've got to meet in the middle of the island. Walk and shout. Watch the depth. Deeper water means you're heading the wrong way."

"Jon!"

Maybe an answer — I wasn't sure.

"Jon!"

"Dad" — faintly.

"Jon!"

"Dad!" — stronger this time.

"Jon!"

And then he stepped into view, as through a partition of heavy Spanish moss. I gave him a quick hug; he looked a bit startled.

"Sorry, sorry, sorry, Jon. I never dreamed this would happen. This is going to wreck everything. This is trouble! Probably serious. We're a long way from shore. Pretty deep water all around. If we step off this island in the wrong place it'll be over our heads. At least it'll be over our waders."

"Dad — "

"Plus the waves could come up. They could come up big time. If we fill our waders with water, then I don't know, I really don't know, especially in water this cold. It's not freezing, but it's cold, and we're a little worn out by now. Cold water in waders is always a problem. Hypothermia is so sneaky. You don't even realize what's happening to you."

"Dad — "

"We can't just stand here. Got to do something. I got to think of something. Just be quiet a second and let me think of something. I'll think of something. Come on now, brain. You usually work faster than this. I got to figure something out; shush, shush, shush, let me see."

"Dad — "

"Huh?"

"Do you remember the directions we took to get out here? Don't you always keep track of directions? I know that when we go for a drive, you get a kick out of asking us what direction we're heading in. And you tease Mom all the time because she never knows the answer. So did you keep track this time?"

"That's something I got from Grandpa — he never really felt comfortable anywhere until he knew where north was. Anyway, on the way out here it was easy since the peninsula runs almost straight from east to west. We walked west out the middle of the peninsula, veered off to the southwest to get to the water, went out almost due south from the shore on that first shoal, hopped to the west to get to that second shoal, and then I gave you the piggyback ride west to the sunken island we're standing on now. But what good does all that do in this soup? Hold out an arm and you wouldn't be able to count the freckles on the back of your hand. Right now it would be stupid to try walking. We could be doing little circles until we collapse. So why ask about directions?"

"Well, I know you think the whole thing is pretty rinky-dink, but I took my wilderness survival kit along again today. Remember?"

"Sure I remember. You've got it in that fanny pack under your waders, right?"

"Right. Safe and dry. And it's got a lot of good stuff in it — "

"Oh yeah — like matches covered in wax so just in case some huge mass of driftwood comes floating by, we can build a little platform and then use the wood that's dry to light such a big fire that it burns through the fog and people can see it from miles away!"

"No, wait. I'm serious. My kit also has a little compass. It's not a great one, like yours — "

"Which is back in the trunk of the car — "

"And I know you always say a job worth doing is worth doing with an excellent tool, but if you don't mind working with a fairly cheap compass, maybe you could borrow mine for a while and use it so we could start moving back over the way we came, go piggyback one more time, and bit by bit work our way back to the shore and finally to the car."

"Well, let's see. I could use it, I guess. Maybe just this one time." ☉

Through All Generations

One of the more significant events of my life occurred when I was only nine years old, and it involved a rowboat, a northern pike, and my dad. This event occurred during what was, for my family, a rather unusual summer vacation. Usually we would pitch our somewhat musty canvas tent with its screened-in porch at a state park somewhere in western or northern Michigan and spend a week or two fishing, swimming, and playing softball on fields with base paths that had long been worn down into sandy ruts. But the summer when I was nine — largely, I recall, because my sister had been born just the prior spring and would, with her high-pitched outbursts during the night, wake up the people in tents so close to our own that we could sometimes hear people snoring in them — we rented a cottage on a small bay of Hess Lake, up near Newaygo.

Along with this cottage came a rowboat. As boats go, this one, I realize now, was nothing special. It was wooden, it was only twelve feet long, and it had a flat bottom. It came with no motor — no fine little outboard, not even an electric trolling motor. Both of its oarlocks were rusty, and one of them had rounded out its socket in the boat's gunnel. Thus if anyone took the boat out for a little row, the oarlocks would creak like sand-hill cranes disturbed at dusk, the oarlock with the bad socket would continually threaten to pop out of the gunnel, and the boat would be in constant danger of being swamped by the wake of a speedboat pulling a skier or two. As nine-year-old boys go, though, I found the boat and the prospect of taking it out fishing on my own one of the better prospects I had ever fantasized about having.

My parents, however, had only to glance at the rowboat lurching around in waves while tethered to the dock, had only to hear from the back porch of the cottage the high-powered speedboats rumbling past and then off along the shoreline, and had only to recall some of the risks that I had already managed to take in the nine years that I had had to work with, and they said I was never to go out in the boat without my dad. And before they issued this rule to me in the presence of my younger brothers and my baby sister, they never consulted with me.

Have you ever seen an utterly forlorn young boy on a dock? In one of my scrapbooks I have a picture that my mother gave me of such a boy sitting at the very end of a dock on a bay of Hess Lake, his upper body slumped over, his left hand support-ing his chin, his right hand slicing the surface of the lake with a reed.

Once I figured out that my moping on the dock was going to have no effect on my parents' decision, however, I decided to make the best use of the boat that I could and started to sit in the back of the boat and fish from it even though it remained tied to the dock. Rarely, I thought then, had the world witnessed someone with so much potential talent having to work within such severe limitations.

I flipped my bobber and worm around the aluminum supports of our and the neighbor's dock and near every clump of weeds growing in the shallow water within ten or fifteen feet of the back of the boat. Occasionally I would take the hook and bobber off my line, tie on a three-inch red and white spoon, and throw that out as far as I could, perhaps once in a while getting the spoon out into five-foot depths. As I brought the spoon wiggling enticingly back to the boat, I even did figure eights with it just below the surface; I had once seen a guy on TV catch something that looked almost prehistoric from a northern Wisconsin lake by doing a brisk figure eight right off the side of his boat.

I often had dozens of minnows follow the big spoon in, competing with one another to nip at it before darting off, but I never caught anything other than weeds with it, and the only fish I ever caught with the bobber and worm were some stunted bluegills and perch — fish five or six inches long, fish so short and thin that after I cleaned them, nothing much was left to eat, a few slivers of meat that perhaps could be fried up and used as hors d'oeuvres, provided, that is, that my parents could make my brothers and sister understand and appreciate a meal served in distinct courses.

I had watched enough television programs about fishing to know where the big fish were. They wouldn't be swimming around the thin supports of seasonal docks, at least not in the daytime, when they would be somewhat exposed and could even be bombed by chubby kids launching themselves as cannonballs from the docks. No, the big fish were out farther and in deeper. They'd be lying hidden along the deep-water edge of the weeds. Or they'd be scattered along the ledges of a submerged island out in the deep water of the lake. If the water got really warm, they'd swim around until they found a depression in the floor of the lake, and there they'd stack up side to side.

As our week at the cottage went on, I was proven right. Sometimes after supper the friend or uncle who was visiting that day would hint to my dad that they should go out fishing for a while, and they'd untie the boat and row out along the far edge of the weeds. They'd toss Johnson silver minnows into the weeds, retrieve them through the heavy vegetation, and just as the lures broke through the edge of the weeds into the deeper water they'd stop reeling and let the lures flutter toward the bottom. They caught a lot of big bass this way, and they had some strikes that they said were so violent that the "whole boat rocked."

Our neighbors used a different, but equally successful, strategy. They motored slowly around the lake with their depthfinder on, and once they had found the deepest hole in the lake they anchored over it, let down live shiner minnows on treble hooks, and caught four- to six-pound bass. When all these fishermen came back to shore, I sometimes got to hold up one or two of their fish and have my picture taken. I was never sure what kind of expression I should try to put on my face.

With all there was for our family to do at and around Hess Lake, and with most of our relatives — including some we hadn't seen very often in the past — coming up to visit us that week, it was not until the very last day of our vacation that my dad said, "Bill, you feel like going out fishing in the boat with me?" In no more than two or three minutes I was in the boat with the little gear I owned then and was set to cast off.

My dad rowed us out past the weeds and then down along

their edge to the north. We tried a variation of what he and our friends and relatives had done throughout the week: We tied on Johnson silver minnows, tossed them toward shore, and then reeled them back toward us crisply, allowing the bodies of these spoons to nick the weeds as they shimmied along over their tops.

I was sure that we'd have fish on in the first minute or so. In fact, the muscles in the back of my neck were tense with expectation. But not a single fish hit. After about a half hour, though, I felt the boat rock and turned to see my dad with his upper body thrown back, his spinning reel held close to his chest, and the seven feet of his fiberglass pole arcing off into the sky. And it was not a big snag, a father playing a little trick on his son; the pole's throbbing signaled a fish, maybe even a big one. I reeled in my own line as quickly as I could so that my dad would have fewer possible entanglements to worry about.

The fight, however, was not exactly what I had expected it would be. The fish made a couple of short runs away from Dad, but it neither jumped nor swirled on the surface, and for a few seconds it seemed as if my dad had lost it, since all at once his line went slack. My dad soon realized, though, that the fish was swimming straight at us, and he started to take up that slack line so rapidly that he was rapping his knuckles on the edge of his reel as he cranked. When the fish, which by now we could see was a northern pike, spotted the side of the boat, it suddenly changed tactics. It thrashed around on the surface near the side of the boat and managed to pelt my dad and me with drops of water that almost stung. Then it dove straight down through the green weeds and into the muck that had been accumulating on the bottom of the lake for years. And there it sat.

My dad pulled quite hard on the line a couple of times, but he felt so much resistance that he worried aloud about breaking the line or tearing the hook out of the pike's mouth. "Now what?" he asked. And we looked back and forth at each other and at the line disappearing into the water. Then he decided to try something I never would have thought of. He pulled the oar with the bad oarlock completely out of its worn socket, jammed the oar straight down into the weeds, and dredged up a swirling mass of weeds and water and muck and bugs. As we leaned over the edge of the boat and gingerly picked through this mass, we ultimately uncovered our northern pike, lying somewhat docilely enveloped in weeds and looking almost stunned as I managed to slide our net first beneath and then around him.

No matter that this pike turned out to be just twenty inches long, barely legal in Michigan at that time. No matter that pike that size really do not have a lot of meat on them. No matter that neither my dad nor I knew how to clean a pike so as to avoid its y-bones. No matter that we caught no other fish that day. "If anybody ever earned a fish," my dad said, "we earned this one." And then I knew two things as solidly as I have ever known anything: There could be no more exciting form of recreation than fishing. And the best fishing was fishing with my dad.

As I grew older, however, it became increasingly clear to me that fishing was not my dad's first love; in fact, it probably would not even make his top-ten list. On other vacations with friends and relatives, in places where one or more boats or canoes were readily available to us, he would opt to play golf, sometimes even mini-golf, instead of going fishing. And more than thirty years after the summer of our northern pike, after I had bought my own boat, a boat that I ordered with cushioned swivel seats so that everyone could be comfortable in it, he would sometimes go out with me and my three sons, but he would never devote himself fully to fishing.

He'd pull out a plastic bag of newly purchased lures and immediately imagine ways to try to improve them. He'd put on bigger treble hooks, add a plastic tail to a spoon, or use a felt marker to draw in on the side of a lure what he said were the flaring gills of a frightened baitfish. All this creativity, of course, kept him from getting a lure into the water as often as his grandsons and I did, and that kept him from catching as many fish as we did. I can see him now, sitting in the back of my boat with his shoulders hunched over and his glasses pulled down onto his nose so that he could examine closely and work on a lure, changing it so much that it would never be used as its designer intended it to be.

When he wasn't redesigning lures, he would often fidget around checking on switches and fuses and plugs. He seemed happiest when I pointed out to him some minor repair that I needed on the boat. He'd pull out the tool kit and start to putter. He's always been able to fix anything.

I finally admitted to myself that my dad really didn't like to fish. Once we can see clearly, we find that our parents don't always turn out to be exactly what we had once imagined. Thus I realized that putting any pressure on him to go along with my sons and me on a typical fishing trip, with all of us spending three or four days rocking around in my sixteen-foot boat, was not the most profound kindness that I could extend to him.

And I finally learned why my dad did not like to fish. When he was a boy, he once told me, his dad would often take him fishing, but my grandpa's invariable strategy involved anchoring near weeds, baiting a hook with a night crawler, dropping the hook to a point just off the bottom, and — most important of all — waiting.

This strategy had quite a lot to recommend it. If the fish didn't bite, my dad and my grandpa didn't have to expend much energy thinking about what other kind of bait they could use. And they didn't have to hoist the anchor and burn up a lot of gas motoring around the lake searching for other places to fish. If the fish didn't bite, the response was simple: You waited some more and sooner or later the fish would break down and take your offering.

My dad never saw this strategy as exemplifying various kinds of stewardship or the psychological advantage that one species might have over another; he found the waiting in the boat supremely dull and discarded any thoughts that fishing could ever be different from what he had experienced. My grandpa had unintentionally killed for my dad what my dad had unintentionally kindled for me.

Because of this unintentional consequence in my life, when I was younger I often faced some pretty tough challenges with sermons related to Father's Day. After all, I fretted, if earthly fathers were supposed to provide visible reminders of our Father in heaven, then what did it mean that my earthly father didn't truly enjoy spending time with me doing what he had led me to enjoy so deeply in the first place? It seemed like some kind of twisted joke. So whenever I heard my minister starting to talk about fathers, fatherhood, and our Father in heaven, I would focus as hard as I could on the purple swirls in the stained glass windows and force myself to think about other things.

What has helped me recently, though, is realizing that although my dad doesn't really like to fish, he does enjoy being along on excursions with my sons and me, and over the past few years we have through trials and errors worked out a way that we can all spend time on or near the water and relatively near one another. We travel together to Michigan's Upper Peninsula and rent a small cottage on Snows Channel near Cedarville. The resort that this cottage is a part of happens to have one of the larger and more stable docks along the entire channel, and on this dock my dad spends most of his time when we're up north.

He hauls a plastic chair out to the end of the dock and makes himself comfortable. He might toss out a sucker or shiner minnow on a hook and watch for a while to see if anything takes it. But he spends most of his time redesigning lures for his grandsons, cleaning and lubricating jammed or corroded reels, and talking to people who dock at the resort for bait or gas.

Since our trip is such a special occasion, I am willing to take all three boys in the boat with me at the same time. So while my dad is on the dock, I head out with them to fish for pike. All three of them like trolling better than any other kind of fishing, and after we first explored the waters in and around Snows Channel we found that, by following the weed-lined edge of the channel in some places and winding our way around small islands and shoals in other places, we were able to chart a usually productive trolling circuit that takes about twenty-five minutes to complete.

At one point along this circuit, we emerge from behind an island and troll directly across from the dock of our resort. For about forty seconds we can look across the sixty or seventy yards of water between the dock and us and see my dad in his chair. My sons, hoping that their grandpa will look up and wave, put down their rods for a few seconds, stand up, whistle, wave their arms, and shout across the waves, "Grandpa! Grandpa! We're way over here!"

It's not possible for me to jump up and wave since I try to steer the boat as close to the rocky ledges near the island as I can, but not every second demands that I peer over the side watching for ledges and boulders, and so, before our trolling route takes us veering off to the west, I glance up as often as I can and under my breath cry, "Dad!" ✆

Separation Syndrome

Having had several years now to mull things over, I can state what was almost certainly the case that awful spring: It was the trip to inspect boat-launch sites that triggered the trauma in our son Joel.

As I reached my later teens, it was never a car or a snowmobile or a motorcycle that I most wanted but could least afford — it was always a boat. But not until I was more than forty years old did I write something that led to records of royalties rather than requests for reprints. I wrote and revised, several thousand people bought the product, and my publisher started sending me a royalty check every six months. After a couple of checks and some research at local boat shows, during March of that year I was able to buy my own boat, an aluminum beauty called a "fishing machine."

But buying a boat is not the same thing as backing it up on a trailer and launching it. When Gene the salesperson helped me hitch the trailered boat up to our van at the dealership, I realized with the force of something like a punch to a kidney that I had never backed up a trailer. Sure, I had read all the typical driver's education materials about turning the car's steering wheel in the direction opposite of the direction you want the trailer to travel in, getting the trailer started in that direction, and then letting the car follow the trailer where it was supposed to go. But I knew that even cars with computer chips under the hood could not on their own obligingly follow trailers into appropriate spots, and I feared that my reading would not count for much when it came to backing up a trailer myself.

You can probably guess how I got the boat home that day: I drove paying more attention to features of my surroundings than perhaps even a poet could normally endure for more than twenty or thirty minutes. Taking care to avoid all sharp turns, to triplecheck before I ever began angling into another lane, and never to turn into a street or parking lot that I might have to back out of, I managed to avoid any trouble and get the boat safely onto my driveway. There I unhitched it, wheeled it around by hand, and pushed it backwards into the garage.

It looked impressive sitting in the garage. But as my friends reminded me in several ways, I hadn't paid thousands of dollars just so that I could invite them into the garage to admire a boat sitting on a trailer. It belonged on the water. "But where?" I wondered. I didn't want to use a boat-launch site that was so large that a number of people would probably be there to watch me go through fits and starts trying to maneuver the boat and trailer into the water for the first time. At the same time, I didn't want to use a launch area so small that I might have trouble driving in and swinging the car and trailer around to start the whole process.

When I confront such challenges, I normally use a two-stage process to try to cope. First, I worry about all the details grinding around in my consciousness. Then I try to isolate and control each and every one of them. And as part of my effort to control aspects of a possible launch, I persuaded Wanda to accompany me on an outing that I might not have dared propose to her before we were married: driving around checking out several boat-launch areas.

Our son Joel, who was eight at the time, could see no fun for him in my proposed venture, and he begged to stay home, even though his two brothers were at friends' houses and he would be the only one home until we got back. He wanted to ride dirt bikes with his neighborhood friend Nick, and he wheedled so persuasively that finally Wanda and I gave in. Before we left, one or the other of us, I think, told Nick's mom that we might not be back until dusk or a little after. And we have some memory of her saying that if it got dark and we were not home yet, Joel could watch TV or play video games with Nick at their house.

So we locked up the house and drove off. But as is so often the case, if things don't fall apart they take longer than expected. We had gotten off to a good start on the tour, finding launch areas at both Murray and Big Pine Island lakes that I would dare to try. But then I decided that I should check out one last site, the one at Wabasis Lake. There too the site did not immediately scare me off, but as we left the lake and headed home, we were already close to losing the sun. And by the time we got home, we could just barely make out a huddled form on our front steps.

You know who it was. Joel had apparently had a great time riding with Nick near the small swamp along Plaster Creek. But as it grew dark, Nick got fed up with the mosquitoes and decided to head home. Since hospitality is not a virtue that most eight-year-olds cultivate, Nick never thought about inviting Joel to come home with him; he just squashed a mosquito on the back of his hand, licked the blood off his skin, headed home, and apparently reported to his mother that Joel was doing fine. He meant that Joel was landing some impressive jumps with his new bike; she took that to mean that we had come back and had Joel safely in the house with us. After Nick left, Joel tried a few more jumps and then headed home himself. There he was mildly surprised to find all the doors locked. But at the time, that didn't make him fret, and he decided to wait on the front porch, where he could see our car the minute we turned onto the street.

But his time on the porch was longer than he expected it to be. I can't pretend to know all of the forces that began to prey on his mind as he sat there. I do recall that a week earlier he had been jumped by a roaming pack of kids who beat him in an attempt to steal his bike; he managed to fight them off and escape with his bike, but only after being seriously bruised on his face and chest. And I also seem to remember that, during his prior year of school, his class had often focused on the plight of children who had been orphaned by famine and war — "the lost children," he had learned to call them. But who knows what other fears he was facing? All I know for sure is that when Wanda and I got out of the car, Joel never said a word to either of us but made of his body a cast encasing my left leg.

I pulled him up for a hug, rather casually dismissed the intensity of the lock of his arms around my neck, and joked about actually finding not just one place but several places where we could launch the boat, even though it might have taken just a tad longer than expected.

Joel apparently didn't get or appreciate the joke, since he

gave no little snort or throaty chuckle. But at the time I thought nothing of it. In the next few weeks, however, this son — the one who had always been our boldest, the friendliest, the most ready to take a risk, the most eager to explore — began to behave as if parts of him had been cut away. If Wanda was the only one home with Joel and decided that she needed to drive up to the grocery store in Alger Heights, he would drop whatever he was doing and insist on going along. If Wanda and I had school conferences for Joel and his brothers, he would beg to go with us and would putter around in the otherwise abandoned playground until all our conferences were finished, often pressing his face to the windows of various classrooms to make sure he always knew where we were.

It became clear that he did not want to go or be anywhere without one or the other of us being present. He even began asking to sleep on the floor at the foot of our bed, frequently sobbing that he "could never stand to lose you guys." And before he would fall into a sweaty sleep, he usually would ask me, "Why did God let all this happen to me? Why can't things go back to how they were? Please, Dad, please, make it stop."

I told him what I had heard in sermons: "God never promises us that everything will be easy, that we will never be hurt. And there is a purpose in the hurt — only it's one that we can't always understand right away. In the end, though, God will show us how everything works out for our good, our ultimate good."

My words didn't seem to help.

Whether it was ironic or fitting I cannot tell, but Joel's fears deeply affected the fishing that he and I tried to do that summer. He never felt secure fishing out of sight of the launch area. Thus his least favorite place to fish was Spring Lake, which extends tentacle-like off the Grand River into numerous weedy bayous. Whenever the wind would begin to take us around a point and into one of these bayous, Joel would fall inactive and quiet, and I knew that unless I moved the boat back to where he could see the launch site, he would put up his brave resistance for a while but would eventually descend into panic, his body huddled in the boat, trembling against the aluminum.

Probably his worst scare came on a trip with my dad and me to Drummond Island. This was one of the few times that I had been able to persuade my dad to come north and actually spend the time fishing, not golfing or fiddling around on some dock.

The first two days of the trip were great, far more successful than we were used to. We found that we could stay in the big bay on the west side of Drummond and fish in the pockets among rock shoals that were within sight of our rented cottage, all the while catching so many smallmouth bass that we needed to take a break now and then and loosen up our forearms and wrists. As opposed to so many of my earlier excursions, on this trip it felt as if we might in fact be chosen — the right anglers in the right spot at the right time.

By the morning of the third day, all this unexpected fishing success led me to begin speculating about religious matters — I started asking my dad and Joel whether they thought the fishing we were enjoying was like the fishing that we could look forward to in heaven.

Now I should probably admit that the images that many people paint of heaven do not thrill me; in fact, images of masses of people standing in white robes singing without end in golden palaces — no green or blue anywhere to be seen — make me vaguely uneasy. These images seem to be based on people's nearly ecstatic experiences in junior choir. But I always hated junior choir. I have memories of standing next to guys who could sing the bass line while I was still embarrassed to have the crystalline voice of a boy soprano. I also have memories of having an aching crush on the choir director, a crush that was probably close to an unforgivable sin since she was the minister's wife.

But since the fishing was so good, it got me wondering whether we will fish in heaven, and, if so, what that fishing will be like. I generally skip over details like whether fish might bleed when hooked, might have their mouths torn when unhooked, and might even take a hook through an eye and lose some of their vision. I tend to focus more on questions such as the following, which I tossed out for Joel and my dad to respond to: Would we catch a fish on every cast, or would that become boring in some heavenly sense of the word? Would we land every fish that we hooked, or would some monsters jump and throw the hook and leave us with stories full of exaggerated details to tell? Or would exaggeration not be possible or motivated in heaven? Could people do in heaven as people do on earth, that is, could they study lakes and streams and fish and feeding habits and actually become better and better at their sport, finally setting themselves apart from many others as experts? Or would that be a kind of distinction God would not tolerate? Would we always have lakes and rivers that beckoned us but that we never had the opportunity to explore, or in eternity would we be able to fulfill all of our dreams, if dreams or aspirations themselves turned out to be possible? Would we ever experience anything like beginner's luck, or would the concept of luck make no sense?

Around the time we were debating aspects of beginner's luck, I pulled the rope to start the engine so that we could move to a new pocket among the shoals, but the wooden handle on the rope cracked, fell off the rope, and left the rope to disappear within the housing on top of the motor. That left us bobbing amid the shoals without any source of power, since the man who had rented us the boat said that if the motor conked out in the big waters around Drummond, oars wouldn't really do us much good.

I wasn't deeply worried since we were only thirty or forty yards from shore. I knew I could strip down a bit, jump in, and propel the boat by holding on to the stern and kicking. And from the shore we would be able to see where we were supposed to end up since our cottage, although about two miles away across the bay, was still visible. Once on the shore, we could hold up our boat cushions, all imprinted on both sides with the word "HELP!" in bold black letters, and could shout at any boaters who might happen to come within hearing distance.

But Joel did not believe that anyone would ever spot us. He stood up, surveyed the bay, glanced at our silent motor, and began to wail: "No way! No way! No way! No one will ever see us way out here. We're never going to get back. We're going to be lost out here in the middle of nowhere all by ourselves forever!" With that he fell to his knees and managed to get most of his body into the small storage space under the small deck in the bow.

I moved clumsily to the front of the boat, knelt behind him, and tried to reach into that space to hold him, to stroke his head, to try with a hug to bring his trembling down. "We'll be fine, Joel, we'll be fine. We'll figure this out. We'll get off the water safely. Don't worry. This will all seem like a big adventure in a day or two. You'll be bragging about it to your friends! I can almost hear you already." But Joel only wedged himself more tightly into the storage space.

I have felt some pains (infections under fingernails, fingers nearly ripped off by a table saw) and I have talked to other people about their pains (passing kidney stones, giving birth to large babies not presenting correctly), but those minutes kneeling in my boat made me ask myself whether there can be any pain like that of watching your own child suffer and being able to do no more to help than run your hand along the crown of the child's head.

Just as my mind was finding panic harder to resist, the engine sputtered once and then kicked into life. While I was kneeling over Joel in the bow, my dad had decided that he was better equipped to play mechanic than psychologist. So he moved to the stern, took out his needle-nose pliers, managed to snake the pullcord out of the engine housing, fished a huge washer out of his tackle box and tied it onto the end of the cord, and used the cord as it was intended to be used — to start the engine. Then he put the motor in gear, carefully worked his way out of the shoals, and sped off into deeper water.

But he didn't head back to the cottage.

When the engine had started, Joel had not immediately edged back out of the storage space. But as the boat picked up speed and started to thunk roughly against the waves, he backed out and peeked above the bow. Then he noticed that we were not headed back to our dock. "Grandpa, Grandpa, Grandpa! Where are you going? The cottage is way back that way! Can't you see?"

To this day I cannot fully understand where Grandpa got the answer that he did. "West first and then north," he said, "north and way around the top of the island to that little cove on the northeast side. Whenever we've come to Drummond in the past, we've talked about exploring that cove, but we've never dared leave this bay. Well, now I've got a big washer tied to the pullcord, we've got plenty of gas, I've got a good map, and I'm steering the boat. I'm going to catch the biggest smallmouth anyone on this island has ever seen!"

I think that Joel was so surprised to find his grandpa throttling up to head out of the bay that he momentarily forgot his fears and tripped into a question: "You really think it'll be good way up there?"

And then after only the briefest of pauses came Grandpa's voice from the stern, carrying to us against the wind: "Joel, I'm sure it'll be better than all three of us put together can even imagine right now!" ◎

All Sufficient?

Even at the time I knew it was foolish. In fact, I knew it was wrongheaded in many ways, back when I was working hard to teach my three young sons to fish, to wish away their boyhood years and yearn for the time when they could handle necessary fishing chores without my help.

But how regularly they used to strain my patience the few times I dared to take all three of them fishing at the same time. They couldn't tie any kind of reliable fishing knot, and their gaze always wandered as I formed and displayed oversized loops of the simplest knot in a vain effort to teach them. When they would snag their hook on a log or the railing of a moored pontoon boat and ultimately snap their line, they would simply extend the frayed end of the line toward me and say, in those gratingly sweet soprano voices, "I need a new hook tied on, Dad. And could you hurry it up, please?"

Nor would they bait their own hooks. They refused to poke around in the dark moss of our bait box, grab a night crawler, and run a hook through it. It was not that they were squeamish about the slimy residue that they saw crawlers leaving on my hands. Nor did they especially mind the fact that crawlers writhed wildly once pierced by a hook. It was just that a bait seller with a rheumy eye had once told them — before I thought they knew a single thing about sex — that every night crawler he sold was "hermaphroditic."

"'A-maphro-did-it?' — what does that mean?" asked Jon.

"It means," the guy said, bringing his face closer to them, "that every crawler in this can has two sets of sex organs, one male set and one female. Can you imagine what goes on when you put a bunch of them together in a dark space?"

After that, my boys always refused to touch crawlers. So I would bait their hooks and help them cast toward promising spots in the water.

But that wasn't all they needed me for. Whenever they caught a fish, they were afraid to unhook it. Somewhere they had heard how dorsal fins could stab them in the palm and how the gill covers of some fish, especially walleyes, could slice their fingers almost as cleanly as razors. So they would simply raise the tip of their poles high into the air and swing the hooked fish over toward my head.

"Dad, Dad, it's a sweet one, a keeper! Can you get the hook out?"

When they caught a little bluegill or perch, I didn't mind having a fish trapeezing around my head. But sometimes they caught bullheads, fish with three sharp barbs protruding from around their heads, and the thought of one of those barbs poking me in an ear made me tense up each time I heard one of them pulling a fish out of the water.

With all these chores and distractions, I sometimes didn't have much time myself to fish. "I can't wait until they can handle all these things on their own," I'd wish. But I didn't know everything that my wishes, once fulfilled, would bring.

By the time my sons didn't need me to help them fish, they were starting to sound the barbaric yawps of adolescence. And with their adolescence came all sorts of unexpected challenges for me.

These started to show themselves even before I would get our boat in the water. As I backed up the boat on its trailer at a launch site, I asked the boys to stand behind me and shout out whether I needed to swing the trailer to my left or right to get it going straight down the ramp. But when I looked in my rear-view mirror, what I usually saw was three skinny boys, their jeans sagging to the point of showing inches of their plaid boxer shorts, gyrating around on the gravel of the launch site and howling shamelessly that I should "back that thang up!"

Shortly after we got on the water, one would usually challenge the others to a casting contest. Each would snap on the heaviest spoon he could find, and then they would take turns seeing who could cast the farthest. They never seemed concerned whether the spots they cast to were likely to hold fish or not. Once they made a cast, they usually reeled their spoons back in so fast that even a fish determined to sacrifice itself would have had to work hard to catch up with them. Each time they whipped their spoons behind them on their back casts, I cringed a little in fear of having a hook rip its way into the muscles on my neck or shoulders. And when they got into an argument about who had won a round, they thought it perfectly sensible to ask me to move the boat over quickly to where their lures had landed so that they could peer over the boat's edge and try to examine vanishing concentric circles and then make a final judgment.

When they actually fished, they hardly ever used lures as they were designed to be used. If certain lures came with parts that were screwed together, they would disassemble them all and then screw the hind end of one to the front of another, often producing lures that would pop and spit and twirl, all at the same time. They would toss these out, watch the little storms they created in the water, and howl with pleasure.

If lures couldn't be disassembled, they added assorted materials to them. They would tie shiny little Mylar skirts onto plastic frogs and glue trimmed seagull feathers onto floating minnow baits. The stranger each invention looked, the happier they were.

Whenever the fishing was a little slow, they tried their own kinds of chumming. They tossed salted sunflower seeds into the water and then cast small poppers right into the oily skim the seeds gave off on the surface. Or they would crack up spicy Doritos, throw them on the water, and then flip jigs with orange twister tails into the middle of them.

The shock for me was that fairly often their pranks produced fish. Once Joel and Jason each caught a five-pound smallmouth bass during a casting contest, when they landed spoons on the shady side of some boulders thirty yards from where I was anchoring the boat in a small bay of northern Lake Huron. And another time Jon caught a forty-inch pike when he tossed his apple core off the stern of the boat, waited a bit, and then plopped a spinnerbait nearly on top of it.

I suppose I should have been happy for them, but to me this was deeply disturbing. It wasn't that they sometimes caught bigger fish than I did. It was the fact that they caught any fish at all. They never worked hard at their fishing. In fact, they put hardly any effort into it. Plus, they followed no traditional guidelines, they did nothing in any standard way, they ignored everything that other fishermen considered conventional wisdom. They would pull their wild stunts and find every part of them hilarious. As far as I could tell, to them fishing was just play, play, play.

"Hey, can we help it we're good?" they would cackle.

But to me they hadn't earned the right to catch any fish. And this made me brood.

"Sure," I thought, "we should always be happy for gifts, pleasant surprises, serendipity, and play. But if we look deep within ourselves, and if we dare to say out loud what we really believe, wouldn't most of us say that at the core of the universe are forces that will eventually reward above all else human discipline, energy, work, and effort? Wouldn't we say that in the most profound sense having to earn things is just?"

If people would listen, I would brood out loud. Once I described my feelings to one of my friends, a retired chaplain. He listened, thought for what seemed an unusually long time, and then mused, "Maybe pure play and delight are simply irresistible — to everything. Maybe play is at the center of the universe."

"I think you're stretching," I replied.

"Well, then," he went on, "when you look at the world, do you typically see a lot of evidence of plain old grace or hardly any?"

"Some."

"And do you think you're able to say exactly to whom it extends and how it shows itself in every case?"

"Not really — but extending even to a small pack of teenagers constantly fooling around?"

"Perhaps especially to them."

"Boy oh boy oh boy! — do you know how hard I'll have to work to bring myself to believe that?" ☙

Brothers Forever

"So was it worth hauling the boat all the way down here? We passed a load of lakes up there around Yankee Springs, you know, and I saw quite a few public access signs. What do you think now that you've been on the water a while?" Joel asked. He was the only one of my three sons who could fish with me that day in late July about two years ago, the day I had decided to try Pine Lake for the first time.

"So far this lake is lobbying hard for a spot on my Top-10-in-Southwest-Michigan List. The largemouths here obviously haven't figured out all the tricks we know, and that pike was a bonus. Plus this is a great example of my favorite type of lake." I meant that it was large and complicated, the kind of lake that for the first couple of hours makes you worry just enough about finding your way back to the launch site at the end of the day that you force yourself to remember and relate a series of landmarks. So far I had stored images of the island cottage with a fifteen-foot lighthouse on its beach, the water tower over the state vocational institute, the guano-covered plastic owl on a spring in the middle of a carpeted swimming dock, and the startling sight of a small stream somehow appearing from under the deck of a modest cottage on a ridge and then cascading down the slope of the front lawn to the waterline.

The blurb I had read about the lake said that it was made up of four different basins. We were in our second one, I figured, and so far both basins had shown us lots of small bays with extensive mats of lily pads, several canals cut into the shoreline and angling back into the dark under willows, and occasional rocky spits that hooked out into the lake, disappearing on a slope into the dark and then jutting up to cut the surface twenty yards farther on. The main basins were connected by channels, most of which wound so tightly between sand flats and gravel bars that they had buoys every ten feet along both sides.

Since the channel we were approaching looked chalky, I decided it was probably so shallow that I should raise the outboard and use the trolling motor to take us through. As that motor hummed us steadily to the far side, I noticed a small wooden boat off to our right, rocking somewhat unsteadily in a finger of water between a sweep of pencil reeds and what was visible of the crown of a giant cottonwood that had been blown over into the lake. In the boat were three young boys, whom I first took to be triplets. All three were strapped into bulky life vests, all three were wearing sunglasses with oversized purple rims, all three had the same light skin, and all three had their hair buzzed down so close to their scalp that the only remaining styling option would be shaving.

As we swept around them on the deep-water side, though, I saw that they were almost surely brothers but not triplets, brothers about as close in age as biology made possible and parental fortitude allowed. The biggest one, who was likely on the verge of fifth or sixth grade, was standing in the middle, reaching one way but turning to look the other. He was sweeping his left hand around, trying to catch hold of the fishing line of the littlest brother, the one in the front, who had snagged his line on one of the reeds and whose tugs on the line were making the reed jerk spastically in the water. He was turning to look to the stern, where the middle brother had stowed his fishing gear and was adjusting the tilt on the trolling motor so that they could power up and move.

While we were still easily within hearing range, the biggest brother hissed to the rear: "Wait a second, James, you goober! Can't you see that Josie has his line snagged? Give me a chance to help him. We shouldn't move until we get his snag out. He can't just go around breakin' off lures all day long."

"Nooo!" the youngest one broke into a whimper. "This is my last purple worm, and if I lose this one, too, I won't have anything left to fish with. All the lures I bought with my mowing money will be lost in the lake!"

It was then, just as a mix of potent emotions was pushing those three brothers toward a fight, a fight in a boat that looked as if it would be somewhat unstable even when everyone was sitting down and trying to stay still, that it occurred to me: After more than forty years, forty years that should have provided opportunity after opportunity, forty years that should have made it probable, even certain, I could not remember a single time that I had been in a boat fishing with both of my brothers at the same time.

Since I have always loved helping others learn how to do things, since I was never more than normally ashamed of or bored with my brothers, and since I thought it only natural that my own flesh and blood should come to love what I loved, this seemed impossible. No way, I thought; there's no way I never took them out in our family's canoe to spots that I knew held fish and helped them fight some big ones and told stories full of near-lies afterwards. I hated to think that my memory was actually failing as fast as my sons sometimes joked it was. ("It's those soy nuts," they liked to cackle. "Lower your cholesterol but zap your brain cells.") I briefly reviewed the two or three family vacations that I could remember best and still could not call up one image of Bob, Bruce, and me together in a boat.

When I was young, our family seemed to form itself in two distinct stages. First my mom and dad had the boys, three of us, one after the other, with two years between me and Bob and another two years between Bob and Bruce. For quite a while, we boys defined the family in terms of ourselves: "Yup, there's three kids in our family — Billy, Bobby, Brucie — three in a row, three little Dutch boys with the same blonde hair, freckled skin, and big feet. We even have the same kind of bellybutton!"

But then, five years after Bruce was born, our parents surprised several people, including us, and we had to do some quick and thorough redefining. One morning late in the school year, Dad didn't just holler at us from the base of the steps to wake us up; he came upstairs, stood by our three beds lined up next to one another, and woke us by squeezing our ankles. While we were moaning in protest and muttering about what usually happened to those who invaded our territory, he said that the night before, after we had fallen asleep, Hazel from next door had come over to stay in our house while he took Mom for a ride to the hospital.

"The hospital? Blodgett Hospital?" We were all suddenly alert. "Why the hospital? What happened to Mom? What time was that, anyway? Is she home now? Is she all right? We never heard a thing. Why didn't anyone wake us? Why didn't we get to go along?"

"She's still in the hospital, but she's fine, just pooped out. Being in labor for a few hours will do that to you, you know. Anyways, we'll be setting another plate on the table now — you all have a new baby sister, Barbara Jean."

"We do? A little Barbie? That makes four B's. So are you gonna hand out cigars all day? Really? OK, so, since we don't smoke, could we maybe have a nickel to spend after school at Popma's? Cigars cost more than a nickel, don't they?" I was alert enough to be cagey.

"A nickel? Three boys and three nickels? Are you kidding me? Today's so special you can each have a dime!"

So each of us had enough money to do something we had never been able to do before: buy two packs of baseball cards at one time. A few days later our little sister came to sleep in a crib in the room where we had always kept the TV and the radio. We had to move our modest family entertainment center to the basement.

Having Barb around changed lots of things in our family, but it didn't change the fact that I was the oldest child. And it didn't change the fact that the three of us brothers usually thought of ourselves as a kind of unit, a special small band within the family, with great skill in almost everything associated with the outdoors, from making camps to catching crayfish. Remembering this made it even harder for me to believe that the three of us had never been fishing together in a boat.

As Joel and I cast near the pontoon boats and under the docks along the shoreline stretching away from the three brothers — we had decided that we wouldn't be able to stop a fight even if it was our place to try, and the brothers were in such shallow water that nothing more than a soaking would come from some pushing and shoving — it came back to me that at least one brother, Bob, and I had fished together, especially before we made it into our middle teens.

I usually tell people that Bob is two years behind me, but when I was young, it always felt like less than that to me. In fact, it always felt as if he was trying to gain on me.

As a boy, he was never as tall and broad as I was, but he was stringy strong and as determined as a sprung trap. And he always wanted to measure his capabilities out, to see how he stacked up against others, to compete. Even with this competitive spirit, however, he was never really hostile, mean-spirited, or overly aggressive. Some deep part of his personality, a part that I have always been secretly envious of, drove him to want to know whether others could do the things he liked and perhaps do them better than he could. If they turned out to be better than he, that same part of his personality drove him to try to figure out what he could do to match and eventually surpass them.

When he was only four or five years old, he started doing push-ups, shirt and socks off in the living room, arms and legs extended on the carpet, bony butt in the air. Fifteen and twenty push-ups at first, up to eighty-six at his peak. He kept a big chart on the headboard of his bed. And he was always pestering me about how many I could do. But when I was young, the rest of my body was always too long and heavy for my arms; I thought I would be able to fly from our upstairs window to the peak of the garage before I would be able to do push-ups or pull-ups or, worst of all, rope climbs. I always told him he didn't even want to know how many push-ups I was doing, working out in the basement when he was away from home.

A year or two after he started his push-ups, he saw an arm-wrestling contest on Wide World of Sports and started challenging me to matches. I couldn't avoid all of these and still walk around with any pride, so we would line up elbows on the kitchen table and start straining against each other. Sometimes Mom figured out why we were grunting and hurried in with worries that we would kick a chair over or smash some of the porcelain lighthouses she displayed on a shelf near her spice rack. When we first did some arm wrestling, I could usually beat him, but then he started going off to the garage for some exercises with pipes, and gradually his wrists and forearms seemed like twisted cables. After a while I could barely budge his arm — if I pressed really hard, he would merely flex his wrist back a little bit — and before I was even ten years old I was finding all sorts of ways to stall, to put him off, to divert his attention. "What's he trying to prove?" I wondered.

On family vacations, Bob and I often fished together in the canoe my dad had gotten cheap from Sidney across the street. Our favorite place, probably, was Lost Lake, just east of the Beechwood loops at Ludington State Park. This is a mostly shallow lake with lots of hidden lagoons where we could tuck ourselves in out of the wind and hope no snapping turtles would rise silently from the muck and attack us.

In some ways, Bob wanted to be just like me as a fisherman.

At least he wanted to have the same fishing equipment I did. One Christmas, Mom and Dad gave each of us a tackle box and a spinning combo, and after Bob noticed that his gear was slightly different from mine, he moped around to the point that he threatened to disrupt family meals. Eventually Mom and Dad brought his equipment back, taking a loss in the exchange, and got him the same kind of brown tackle box and baby-blue rod as I had. Whenever I saved up my allowance and bought a new lure — as a kid I loved Hula Poppers, especially the red and white ones — he would head out bottle hunting, turn his finds in for a refund, and then go out and buy an identical lure, taking care to show me as he stowed the lure in his tackle box.

When we fished together, though, he never tried any tactics other than those he had come up with on his own. In clear-water lakes, I often liked using blue or brown tubes, and if I found that smallmouth roaming the dark side of drop-offs were probably seeing these as crayfish and were sucking them off the bottom almost as fast as I could get them down there, I would tell Bob to switch to a tube and cast it where I was. I would even show him the erratic twitches I was using on the retrieve.

He always refused. He acted almost as if I had insulted him. No, thank you very much, he didn't think of it first so he would try a different lure and find something that would work even better than what I had come up with. And he tried. Almost manically. But I would go on catching fish, and he only grew more frustrated. After a while, he would tie on something else, and when that didn't work either he would want to move to a new place. "Move?" I would respond. "Why move? The smallmouths here are trying to break my wrist!" Soon he asked to beach the canoe so that he could switch places with me and sit in the back and run the small Mercury outboard my dad had clamped to a panel; he wanted to be the one picking out spots.

Even after I let him run the motor and decide where we would go, though, he was never content to stay in one place very long. It got to the point that there was always a new spot that he could imagine, a spot a little farther on, a spot more inviting than anything we had seen. Each point called for him to come around it; each channel beckoned him in. He had become a fisherman in a hurry. Push this a little further, I thought, and you're just out riding around on a lake.

When he was only thirteen, he decided that it was time for him to have his own boat, and, calculating that it would take him more than a year to save up for one on his own, he decided to send away for some boat-building plans. Some people talk about sending for plans. Some people send for the plans and then leave them mixed in with other papers. Some people use the plans to make a token start on a project and then abandon it. But Bob, occasionally having to ask my dad for advice, really built his own small boat, sawing, filing, clamping, gluing, sanding, painting, and varnishing through most of a summer, while the only thing the rest of us kids on the block built was an unstable backstop for our baseball field. After Bob had his own boat, and after he made a few adjustments to it so that it didn't list a little to port, he and I never fished together again. The boat wasn't large, but it was a two-seater, and I thought I could fit my legs in the front, but Bob said that he didn't want anyone in front of him blocking the view. He would use his boat; I could have the canoe.

"Think about this a minute, Bob," I used to argue. "We'll probably have more luck if we fish together. We'll figure out parts of lakes faster; we can discuss strategy as we go along. And just think of all the stories we'll be able to tell together, you taking a part, then me adding to it, then you going on about that. We're brothers — don't you think brothers should stick together?"

"We can cover a lot more territory if we go separately," was the only response he ever gave me.

People must have wondered about our family as we drove to vacation spots after that. Six of us scrunched into our old Plymouth Fury, we three boys practically fighting to avoid the hump in the middle of the floor in back. We strapped the canoe onto car-top carriers, we towed our pop-up trailer behind the car, and on top of the pop-up, in a cradle that my dad and Bob designed and built, we transported Bob's boat.

As Joel ponged his tube off the float of a pontoon and almost immediately had a strike from a good bass, I realized that my memory about the details of my boyhood was getting clearer and clearer. Probably, I thought, I should have kept up the pressure on Bob to join me in the canoe once in a while or to let me go out in his boat with him. But around the time he started using his boat, Mom finally said that Bruce was old enough and big enough to start going out in the canoe.

I usually tell people that Bruce is about four years behind me, but when I was younger, it always felt like more than that to me. In fact, it seemed as if he was always off at a distance.

I remember him being the one told to shag all the foul balls during neighborhood baseball games, wading around looking for shells in the shallow water when all the other kids were on the raft in the deep, coasting down the bunny hill when Bob and I were trying to take jumps on the steep slopes while standing up on our sleds, watching through the chain-link fence as Bob and I skidded around turns on go-carts. Even now, so many years later, Bruce will tell me stories about his childhood and adolescence and I have to study him closely to see if he's kidding or not: "You ran cross-country in high school? Really? Was I still living at home then?"

Compared to Bob and me at any given age up to about eighteen, Bruce was always shorter, thinner, more gentle and tender. Bob and I would wrestle and shove each other around, sometimes knocking vases off tables; Bruce sought the quiet in places and places with quiet. Before and even after Barb was born, Bruce was the one the rest of us in the family reminded ourselves we had to look out for; he was the one who was always getting hurt.

All of the kids in the neighborhood loved playing tap football in a field made up of our front yard and the Slobins', next door. Most of us could run straight to our maple tree, cut to where the sidewalk from the Slobins' porch met their driveway, and then sprint on an angle and catch a pass just before going out of sight past the corner of their garage. When Bruce was first told to run that pattern, he sprinted on a sharper angle than he should have, stretched out both arms for a somewhat overthrown pass, and put both of his arms right through the window of the Slobins' garage. This made a mess of the window. He then made a mess of his wrists and forearms when, in a reflex, he jerked his arms back sharply over the splinters of glass. They ripped through his muscles and tendons and nerves almost down to the bones.

Later, Mr. Slobin took a close look at his broken window and said that Bruce had left little chunks of flesh on the splinters.

With that accident Bruce set the record in our family for stitches, and he probably also set the record for necessary attention and therapy afterwards. After the stitches came out, Dr. Hillman said that people should help Bruce move his arms and hands, especially his left arm and hand, through a wide range of motion; otherwise, he warned, Bruce might never again be able to do normal things, like grip and swing a baseball bat. Dr. Hillman also said that Bruce's scars should be rubbed with ointment, some kind of vitamin E oil, so that those scars wouldn't stick up and mark him so badly. Mom did most of this, but Dad also took a turn, and Grandma Fannie and some of our aunts helped out whenever they were around. For quite a while there, Bruce often had people hovering around fussing over him.

If Bruce hadn't been so accident prone, maybe Mom would have let him come out in the canoe when Bob and I were still fishing together in it. But even though she didn't release Bruce until after Bob was off charging around in his own boat, I was pleased. To have a paddler in the front of the canoe would make things easier for me, especially in the wind, and no experience with Bob had stopped me from wanting to share my love for fishing.

So Bruce and I paddled out one humid August day to a bay of Lost Lake that had somewhat deeper water just off its mouth. I rigged up his line with a bobber, tiny sinker, good-sized hook, and a chunk of night crawler. He gave several signs of being a fast learner. After only two or three tries, he learned when he should release his line to make a good cast. He never left his line falling behind him or pummeled the surface of the water a couple of feet in front of the canoe. And once he had his bobber floating on the surface of the water, he seemed remarkably patient. Never once did he ask to move, and he hardly ever wiggled around in the canoe; he seemed to have some deep stillness in him.

As I watched him more closely, though, I started to wonder how good of an angler he was going to become. Most of the time he really wasn't focusing on his bobber; several times I noticed that his bobber was dipping and swaying around in tight circles, but he didn't notice it. He would be staring down into the water, watching weedy arms flow sinuously in subsurface currents, counting shiner minnows schooled up tight to the roots of stumps, trying to trace the apparently aimless trails of snails on the bottom.

"Bruce," I would whisper, "you just missed a bite. You gotta watch. All the time. You can't just take a glance at your bobber every thirty seconds or so. The fish are gonna steal all your bait."

"Don't you worry, big brother. I'm not after those little nibblers. I'm waitin' for the big papa, the one that will take all my bait in and swim off with it. He'll think he's had a free meal, but I'll show him that he picked the wrong guy to fool with."

It didn't happen right away, but after about fifteen minutes — during which I had caught two small bluegills and a pretty good perch — Bruce's bobber moved steadily away from the canoe toward some large lily pads and then disappeared under the water.

"Gonna get this one?" I asked. "Or you handing out another free meal?"

"You better hold on tight," he said as he raised a hand to

hush me. "No one thought I could do it, but I'm gonna start off with Mr. Big Daddy himself. I just need to give him time to get it all in his mouth — that was a pretty big chunk of night crawler." With that he set the hook, and almost immediately afterwards a largemouth bass, probably not quite big enough to keep but coming into some serious strength nevertheless, jumped and shook its head violently, trying to spit the hook. But Bruce kept good pressure on the line, and the bass fell back into the water, still hooked. It then powered its way off toward the mouth of the bay, where it found a huge mass of weeds floating on and just below the surface and disappeared into it. The rod I had given Bruce to use had twenty-pound test line on it, and he hauled back and hauled back and reeled as much as he could, the drag whining occasionally as he reeled, eventually getting the bass and another couple of pounds of weeds that the fish had surrounded itself with close enough to the canoe that I could net the whole mess.

As we picked through the weeds and finally uncovered the fish, Bruce started shouting, "I did it! I caught a fish! A monster. Maybe the biggest of the day. Maybe even of the week. I wish Mom and Dad could have seen that!"

"It probably is the best of the week so far. It's bigger than anything I've caught, that's for sure. And it's bigger than anything Bob's caught up to today — we'll have to wait to hear how he did this morning. Now let's see how hard it's gonna be to get the hook out."

When we pried the fish's mouth open, I could see that the line went straight down its gullet; the hook was out of sight, deep within the bass. Bruce had given it way too much time with the bait.

"I don't know about this, Bruce; the hook is down so deep I can't even see it. I can pull on the line to see if it gives at all. If it doesn't, we've got ourselves a problem. I'm pretty sure this fish isn't long enough to keep, so we're gonna have to try to release it alive. Let me try a tug. Ah, shoot!"

The hook was firmly embedded, probably well along the way to the fish's stomach. Even my light pull on the line brought blood from the fish's throat, through its gills, and onto my hands.

"Bill!" Bruce's voice was up high. "Stop it, stop it, stop it! Don't make it bleed. What did you have to make it bleed for? You're gonna kill it!"

"Shaah! Don't even start that! You're the one who gave this fish half the afternoon to swallow your bait. That night crawler's probably digested by now. I'm just trying to think of a way to get us out of this mess. There's no way I can pull that hook out. And if I stick a pliers down its throat, that'll tear everything all up. The only other thing is to cut the line and leave the hook in the fish. I've heard that after a while they digest the hook. I guess I'll try that — I can't think of anything else."

So I cut the line as close to where it disappeared into the fish's throat as I could, and then we held the bass upright in the water next to the canoe, swishing water gently back and forth through its gills. It seemed to be working; I could feel some twitching coming back into the muscles near its tail.

"OK, Bruce, we've got to try. Let it go. We'll see if it makes it."

Bruce gave it a little push, and it swam off weakly for a few feet, fighting the tilt, and then it went over completely on its side and floated on the surface.

"It's gonna die," Bruce whimpered.

"Maybe not; let's row over and try reviving it again. It's still got enough strength to splash around on the surface."

We went through this process several times, holding the bass upright in the water, swishing water through its gills, giving it a little shove, and then watching as it struggled off away from us but then eventually came up on its side. As it made its strongest attempt to stay upright and swim, moving out desperately eight or ten yards, a shadow passed over us, and a gull landed between us and the fish, pushed the fish away from us, and started to peck at it.

"Beat it, you garbage bird! Come on, fish, swim away, swim away now! Get away from that gull!" Bruce shouted as he looked for something in the canoe to throw. He found a few sinkers, but he couldn't keep them concentrated, and as they bit the water in a loose pattern around the gull, the bird turned back to the bass and pecked out one of its eyes.

"No! No! My fish . . ." Bruce had to turn away.

"Come on," I ordered; "grab your paddle. We're heading back to camp. Right now. We're not watching any more."

But he just slumped over in the front of the canoe, his shoulders heaving. It took me a long time to paddle us back to shore.

When we got back to our campsite, he climbed into the back seat of the car and lay there on his stomach, his feet sticking out the half-open door. Once I explained to Dad and Mom what had happened, they told me to leave him alone — that would not be the only nasty thing he would ever have to see in his life. Dad would talk to him once he settled down. He would get over it eventually, they thought.

And maybe he did. But as far as I know, after that day he never fished again, with me or anyone else. One afternoon. One short excursion in the canoe. One gut-hooked fish. The cutting off of so much future.

"It's true. It never happened," I murmured to myself.

"What's that?" Joel shot back. "Talking to yourself again? Pretty soon you're gonna need a personal attendant." We could no longer even see where the three boys had been fishing off the edge of the pencil reeds.

"Sorry. A little preoccupied, I guess. Those young boys way back there along the shoreline, those three brothers, got me wondering whether my two brothers and I have ever spent time together fishing in a boat. I realized we haven't. And now I can't just let it sit. I'm gonna have to try to set something up."

"You are? With Uncle Bob and Uncle Bruce? Do they even like to fish? Have they ever gone? I don't think I've ever heard them say a word about fishing. And they're as busy as anybody. You might be setting yourself up for a new Paul Simon song — 'still disappointed after all these years.'"

"Maybe. Bob left me on my own and took off in his own boat when we were kids. Not too long after that Bruce went out with me once and got freaked out. But that was about forty years ago — a lot can change in forty years."

"Sure. But can you change who a person is? If something hasn't happened in forty years, maybe it's not meant to happen."

"Yeah, well, you know me — I never really learned all my lessons about accepting things."

That was late July. "Why not try to set something up for next spring?" I said to myself. That would give me plenty of time to think of a prime spot. And that would give me plenty of opportunities to try to persuade Bob and Bruce, in case one or both of them claimed that they couldn't afford time for a fishing trip with brothers. "You've spent half your life reading about rhetoric; it's about time you see if it works in the real world!" I told myself.

My first challenge was to get Bob and Bruce to pull themselves away from their wives and kids for a day or two. For this to happen, I decided, our destination had to be north, probably in the Upper Peninsula. As kids, the three of us had always loved family trips across the straits — first on a huge car ferry and later over a bridge on which we dared one another to stick heads out the window and look down through the metal grating. Plus, as adults Bob and Bruce had backpacked throughout both the Hiawatha and the Ottawa national forests.

My second and perhaps greater challenge was to get them to spend some of our time away fishing. As I mulled this over, I remembered a spot that Bob had mentioned to me once while we were rummaging through reprints in the dusty library of the biological station he works for. He had mentioned that Chase Salmon Osborn, a former governor of Michigan, had deeded to the bio. station a large tract of land on Sugar Island, which lies in the St. Mary's River south and east of Sault Saint Marie. On this tract were buildings that Osborn had used to entertain guests; one of these was a large cabin with a bunkroom, a kitchen, and a sitting room with fieldstone fireplace. This cabin, Bob had added, was available to rent for a surprisingly low fee.

"An island," I thought. "What could be better for a fishing

trip than that? I hear it's even got extensive swamps in the interior. So what else is there to do but fish? And maybe I could challenge Bob and Bruce to plan on catching most of what we eat for at least one supper. Each of us can bring our own drink and some dinner rolls, but we'll have to catch fish for the main course. The fear of even modest hunger pangs can be a strong motivator. Why'd I have to get so old before I got so smart?"

Finally, I had to get the three of us fishing together in the same boat. I don't usually tow my boat more than an hour or so away from home, but in this case, I decided, I would tow it all the way to the Soo. It had plenty of room for all three of us, and I decided to install two new seats, with adjustable supports, so that Bob and Bruce could sit in comfort.

Once I e-mailed Bob and Bruce with my proposal, they surprised me: no questions, no cautions, no adjustments, no refusals. Both of them, they said, could imagine such a fishing trip up north. But neither could get away for more than a couple of days.

"That's fine," I e-mailed back. "I'll look for a date after the bass opener in the U.P. How about if we show up late afternoon one day, fish most of the next, and then head home the morning after that? Even in that short time, we should be able to find some fish. At least we should if we want more for supper than a bunch of rolls."

"Let's do it," they both e-mailed back, adding some bragging about how it would take more than what a U.P. island had to throw at them to make the Vande Kopple brothers go hungry. I set a date and arranged to rent the cabin.

During the following winter, I spent more than my usual amount of time in tackle shops. I had never fished around Sugar

Island, but I had been to Drummond Island, south of Sugar at the mouth of the St. Mary's River. If the fishing around Sugar was similar to that around Drummond, we would probably find smallmouth, walleyes, and pike. So I tried to prepare for all these possibilities: I bought in-line spinners and small minnow baits for the smallmouth, crawler harnesses and jigs for the walleyes, and spoons and spinnerbaits for the pike. And I bought triples of most of these lures. My deepest hope, the one I never dared admit to myself more than once a day, was a re-make of a scene from *A River Runs Through It*: One of the lures I had brought would be the magic bait, Bob and Bruce would notice my repeated success, they would ask if I happened to have any more of that kind of lure, and I would pretend to rummage around in my tackle box and then say that I just happened to have a couple that they could try.

About a week before it was time to head north, I e-mailed them to let them know that, since our van was set up to tow my boat, I would drive. I proposed to pick Bruce up in Grand Rapids, travel together up to the bio. station near Pellston, pick Bob up, and then drive together the last hour to the Soo.

But Bruce said that, before traveling the last miles to the Soo, he wanted to check out a new set of hiking trails in the dunes west of St. Ignace; he would drive on his own, and he'd be leaving earlier than I could get away. And Bob said that he probably should drive on his own, too; he needed his car for some special equipment he wanted to bring.

"Not very thrifty — especially for a bunch of Dutchmen," I thought, "but at least I know they can both find their way."

So I drove on my own to the Soo, found a little park south of the power plant where I launched my boat and parked the van, and headed south in the river. Once I reached the island, I took quite a bit of time to check the water, using the trolling motor to explore coves and rock shelves all the way down the west side, around the southern tip, and then a third of the way up the east side to the little bay with a cabin flanked by a red pine with its crown blown off. I had almost lost the sun, but I wanted to have a good idea of spots to try during our one day of fishing.

After I hauled my gear up the slope to the porch of the cabin, I found Bob and Bruce arranging supplies in the kitchen.

"Hey, guys," I said, "still finding your way around, huh? Great to see you. I can't believe this is actually working out for all three of us. I would have been here earlier, but I put in some time checking on spots for tomorrow. A lot of territory looks really good. Am I ready to get out there! So all the way up here I've been wondering — what kind of equipment did you guys bring to fish with?"

"You can't believe the rod Bob has. It's telescopic. Comes in a case about two feet long — you could fit it in a suitcase — but then you take it out, slide out the sections, and you have a fishing pole about five feet long."

"A telescopic rod? Where'd you ever find that?"

"I saw an ad for it in a travel magazine," Bob chuckled. "It takes up hardly any space on a trip, and once you get all the sections pulled out, it's pretty flexible and still strong. With as much fishing as you do, I'm surprised you don't have one. Keep it in the trunk for that gorgeous little stream you stumble on."

"Maybe I should get one. A lot of the hotels where I stay for conventions have ponds on the property, and most of them look pretty bassy. OK, so Bruce, how about you?"

"Well, mainly I brought our new camcorder, so if anybody hooks something, I can make a film for everybody to see at Christmas. If we do find lots of fish, I thought I could borrow one of your poles, Bill, since you say you keep four or five ready to go in the boat."

"Six for this trip. You're welcome to my new spinning rod. I'll show you how to use it in the morning."

"Speaking of the morning," Bob cut in, "I think we should skip the card games and big talk tonight and get to bed as soon as possible so we can get an early start tomorrow. We're all set up for a big day, right?"

"That's about the best idea I've heard all spring," I said, and within fifteen minutes we were all rolling out sleeping bags on bunks.

When I went to the kitchen in the morning, only Bruce was there, finishing a box of raisins after his Cheerios.

"Bob up yet?" I wondered. "After his pep talk last night, he sure shouldn't be sleeping in."

"Bob? You kidding me? He's been up for more than an hour. Got up, ate, packed himself some bread and oranges for lunch, and took off in his kayak."

"His kayak? He's got a kayak? You gotta be kidding me!"

"Nope. Guess that's why he wanted to drive himself. He's got this nifty titanium carrier on his car. He and a couple of his friends at the station have gotten into building kayaks. Their best trips so far, he said, have been up in Lake Superior off the Agawa River. Today he's gonna try to make it around this whole island, and if that goes faster than he thought, he might try sliding south and paddling around Neebish Island too."

"He's really got a kayak? Is he gonna fish at all?"

"He took his travel pole, and he said he'd see how the spirit moved him."

"So . . . what about you? You coming out with me? I can be ready to go in fifteen minutes or so."

"I could, if you really want somebody in the boat with you. But Bob said he's heard that there's a tiny island up this coast a ways that's loaded with cormorant nests. I guess everybody up here hates those birds — they think they're eating all the perch, so they shoot 'em if no one else is around. If you're OK going out by yourself, I'm itching to hike up the shoreline to see if I can find those birds. Maybe I can sneak up on them for some pictures."

"What? Oh. OK. I get it. Sure. OK. That's probably a good idea — you won't see many cormorants down around Grand Rapids. But what about supper tonight? Who's gonna catch the fish for supper?"

"Well, you're the fisherman in the family. Never any real doubt about that. At least you're the only one who's always talking about fishing. And even if you get only a couple, we've got enough of this and that so we won't go hungry tonight — at least not really hungry. I've packed some snacks for my lunch. See you later in the day. I don't know how long it's gonna take me to find those birds."

It suddenly seemed as important as anything to read the fine print about how much saturated fat was in a serving of Cheerios.

But still, I thought after a while — I was surrounded by water. And I had hauled my boat five hours up here. I should at least take it out and try. So I went out and pushed it off the beach. Then I headed north up the east side of the island, to where the river opened up into a sizable lake, Lake George. I didn't have much energy.

I soon noticed, though, that the wind was steady out of the northwest. I could make drifts with a crawler harness across the lake, taking care not to drift so far that I floated into Canadian waters. Maybe I could get some walleye. But it was bright, and I suppose they were deeper than I was fishing. All I caught was a few perch, all of which bit almost violently but turned out to be so small that I decided they wouldn't be worth cleaning.

After several hours of these drifts, being pushed to the southeast and then motoring methodically back across the lake, the chop pup-pup-pupping against the bow, I drifted down past a little comma of a peninsula and saw both Bob and Bruce standing on some boulders waving toward me.

"Come on over here," they yelled as I approached. "You can tie the boat up over there. We met up a few minutes ago and were hoping we'd find you — you've gotta see what we found."

I used the mooring spot they indicated, and then rock-hopped up to their level.

"What? What's up? One of you hurt?"

"No. Look over there." Bob pointed inland. "You can't believe this little storage house."

"A storage house? Who needs anything like that up here? Whose is it? And who knocked that big hole in the door?"

"It must have been Osborn's. It's full of stuff with his name on it. Lots of mothball smell. Some vandals must have hacked the hole in the door, and it looks like they did it just this spring — what they didn't take is in pretty good shape yet. Come on in. We've already looked around a little. It can't be wrong just to look."

So we hunched down and stepped through the hole in the door to walk in the half light among oak bookcases and along shelves fastened to heavy block walls. Board games in torn and faded boxes piled on top of one another, Monopoly on the top. Stacks of what looked like personal journals, many with dog-eared pages, and bundles of old envelopes, all with the stamps cut off. A buffalo coat — to wear it was to suffocate, I thought. Several different hats: a top hat with a bent brim, a coonskin hat with just the butt of a tail left, and a beanie that was black on the inside and reddish brown where it had been exposed to the light. Seven pairs of scuffed-up shoes, all with the outside left heel worn down. Pictures of a woman in a long wool shirt, seated on a rock with writing materials close at hand. A twenty-by-twenty room full of the things gathered across the years of a life, most of which things, now that vandals had knocked a hole in the door, had an unobstructed view across the St. Mary's to a stretch of deserted shoreline in Ontario.

We didn't stay very long. And we didn't say much, other than things like, "We'd better go now." "Yeah, we probably should." "Let's get out in the air and light."

Once outside, we agreed that it was time to head back to the cabin and have our supper, slight as it promised to be. I got back in my boat; Bob set off in his kayak; Bruce wanted to double-time it back along the shore.

It turned out, however, that our supper was better than I expected. Each of us had brought a package of dinner rolls, and each package was different from the others, so we had a nice variety of rolls to choose from. Bob had brought some of his homemade blackberry wine. And Bruce had cheated a little: he had stopped in the Soo for a couple of smoked whitefish. Their soft flesh was sharp on the tongue, and the taste stayed on our fingers; long after the fish was gone we could lick a finger and have a savory reminder.

As each one of us took a turn peeling an inch or two of flesh off the backbone of a fish, the other two would wait their turn and watch intently, almost holding their breath, afraid that one might get more than his share. When we realized what we were doing, we looked at one another sheepishly and started to hoot. After a minute, I had to massage the knots out of the muscles behind my ears.

When we had quieted down, Bruce said, "It reminded me of Sunday dinner back when we were kids. Do you remember how Bob would always offer to help set the table after church? And then he would put the beef roast right where he could get at it first. No big surprise that he always got the best piece. And then he would make such a dramatic display of slicing it up while the rest of us were watching him and realizing that all the pieces left were thick with suet."

"Wait one little minute," Bob shot back. "I sent all the vegetables around the back of the table your way. You could have had all the vegetables anybody would ever want."

"No kidding," Bruce responded. "You sent every bean and pea Mom ever cooked my way. I'm surprised I didn't turn green. But 'they're good for what ails ya,' Dad always said, and I had a lot of stuff ailing me."

"And what about Mr. Big Brother here? Don't you think it was just a little suspicious when he would always take Mom and Dad's side about meals we'd have preferred to bag up for the neighborhood dogs? I still remember him saying how liver was supposed to be so good for us. Real people don't actually ever eat liver, do they?"

From there we moved on to a wild tale about the time Bob had to try the biggest dessert the Ludington House of Flavors offered, a Super Pig's Dinner, and how he had had to stop on the way back to camp for an emergency dash into the dunes. We howled about the fact that as Bruce got older there was never a potato at our table that he couldn't eat. "Any given amount," Dad used to say. "Bruce will eat any given amount." And finally Bob and Bruce started in on me for taking Mom's side about beets. "Don't you remember?" they mimicked. "Bill used to say, 'Beets — red beets for healthy blood!' His eyes were changin' to brown!"

As we were cleaning up afterwards, Bruce said, "I've been wracking my brains all afternoon trying to think how long it's been since we took a fishing trip together. I'm having a tough time remembering. I had completely forgotten how great these trips are."

And then Bob said, "Yeah, we probably should have been slipping away for a day or two every year since we got out of college. You're good at setting these things up, Bill. Could you plan another trip for next year, or are you getting sick of chasing all the details?"

I didn't hesitate. "Sure. I'll give it a try for next year again. It's a bit of work, but next year should be easier. Now at least I have a better idea than before about what we're trying to catch." ⑥

A New Earth

"You want me to do what?" I almost choked when, on that drive from Sioux Center, Iowa, where my family and I were visiting several relatives on my wife's side, my sons suddenly asked me to turn the radio off.

Since they earlier had tuned the radio to a Yankton station broadcasting sounds that I was sure could drive night crawlers out of the ground in bright sunshine, I was eager to comply. And when I saw how intently those three boys — ages nine, twelve, and thirteen — were scanning the pavement ahead, watching for and counting off the gravel roads that came up on both sides out of corn and soybean fields and intersected our county blacktop every mile, I guessed what their motives were.

Their Uncle Stan had told them how to find what he called a "secret fishing hole — a little piece of paradise on the prairie."

"Sure," I thought as I listened, "a secret fishing hole right in the middle of land that's been plowed, planted, and fertilized for decades. What kind of joke is he trying to play, sending these wide-eyed city kids off to explore the muddy shallows of some drainage ditch or to try to find a place to stand among fidgety Holsteins on the edge of a watering hole?"

But my sons have special talents for wheedling, and after being stung by their pinched vowel sounds for most of a day, I gave in and agreed to help them try to find what they had started to call their "pondo perfecto."

Once we were on the road, they asked me to turn the radio off for a reason: They wanted no possible sensory overload to keep them from dictating Stan's directions to me word for word and to keep me from following those directions accurately. So we traveled with everyone at full alert — five miles west on the blacktop, then three more miles south on the gravel, then back east on a seasonal two-track until you crest a hill and see the sparkle of the pond in a valley shaped like a broad arrowhead pointed south.

Roughly thirty years earlier, just after we graduated from college, three friends and I had discovered a fishing spot that was as close to perfect as I ever dared to hope to find in this life. For eight hours of one night and a few more hours of the next day, we had driven to Watersmeet on the far west side of Michigan's Upper Peninsula. Then we loaded our gear into two canoes and paddled hard for two hours before setting up camp in an area that was labeled a wilderness tract even on the old maps. The next day we canoed forty minutes away from camp, portaged for almost a half mile, and finally stumbled out of a stand of birch onto the boggy shore of a bay on the south side of East Bear Lake.

The fishing there provided images that still appear in many of my best dreams. From the shoreline of that bay, lily pads extended out into the water fifteen or twenty feet. Once we got our canoes through these pads and floated ten or fifteen yards outside them, we snapped on plastic night crawlers, flipped them onto lily pads along the outside edge, let them sit there for a few seconds, and then twitched them off the pads, watching them fall in slow and sensual undulations. They were irresistible. Largemouth bass were lying in the shade of the pads, and when they saw the worms doing their descending dance, they would flash out and inhale them.

The fights were matters of domain. If the bass managed to take our lines back into the jungle of stalks, they usually got off. But if we managed to keep the bass out in deeper water and had some patience with them, after a while we usually were able to hold them in the air, sing out a few bars from the "Hallelujah" chorus, and stare proudly into a camera lens.

Before we left, we decided to sample at least one other part of the lake, the shoreline on the far north side. There we found a different kind of water and a different kind of fish. On a ridge overlooking this shoreline was a stand of enormous — probably virgin — red pines. Just to the west of these, the glinting waters of a brook raced down to mix among the gravel spits and boulders in the water near the shore. When we flipped tube jigs into the shade of the boulders or jerked them across the gravel, stirring up little trails of sediment, smallmouth bass hit them as if they wanted to hurt them first and eat them later. They were not quite as fat as the largemouths, but they fought as if they had a more serious attitude problem.

Two spots, two great fisheries, and so much of the lake left to explore! Since that trip, my friends and I have tried to stay in touch. When one of us e-mails the others every three or four months, he will often refer to East Bear Lake and the promise we made there to get together while we still had our health and explore the rest of that lake. But we are all so busy. And we have families that do not put hauling canoes along wilderness trails at the top of their things-to-do-on-vacation lists. I'm pretty sure we made a promise we will never keep.

But, I told myself as our van idled high on that two-track in northwest Iowa, it's possible that there are other fabulous fishing spots. And as I looked down on the pond, I began to have a strange sensation. After I got out of the van and followed my sons down into the valley, the sensation intensified. I turned around slowly but could see no barns, no windmills, no silos, no crops, nothing that brought human endeavor to mind. And the grasses surrounding the pond were long and full of wild whispers in the breeze. Could this be a small pocket of pristine prairie, and could this pond be loaded with bass whose genes carried the imprint of prehistoric seas?

My sons broke into my reverie by insisting that I help them rig up their rods.

"What do you want to fish with?" I asked.

"Bobbers and worms."

So we started rigging our rods up with a bobber, a swivel, a small hook, and a chunk of night crawler. And we decided to start fishing from where we were at the northernmost point of the pond, leapfrogging our way down along the west side.

Joel, the twelve-year-old, was the first to cast, and as soon as his bait hit the water, a little storm erupted around it. Slashing four-inch bluegills nearly collided with one another as they hit the bobber, hit the swivel, hit twists and bends in the line, and practically impaled themselves on the hook.

"They must be starving!" Joel yelped.

"Yeah," Jason countered, "and every crazy one of them is only four inches long!"

"No way they can all be that little," Joel shot back. "There's got to be some big mamas in here somewhere!"

But along the entire western edge, all we found was tiny and insanely hungry bluegills. When we came to the south side, we saw the sign:

> This pond has to many littel fish.
> Please catch some and put them in the
> tiling over there → to feed the crick.
> You can help make it great.
>
> Thanx, P. Engelsman

To me, the prospect of helping was powerfully attractive. After all, I thought, if my boys and I couldn't discover a perfect fishing spot, maybe we could play a leading role in creating one.

At the college where I teach, my colleagues and I talk all the time about being God's agents in renewing creation, about working to make all things new. In fact, it is with precisely this language that our college presents itself to the public. But it's not easy for us teachers to affect creation directly and immediately. If we ever succeed, we probably do so indirectly, through the effects of our words on students. And it is possible, perhaps even likely, that they could graduate and be off in Haiti or China or the Bronx renewing creation and we might never hear about it. So thinking about my own chance to do something tangible and immediate to a part of creation, if only a small part, made me both excited and resolute.

"Well," I said to the boys, hoping to channel their energy, "it's not a wilderness treasure, but maybe we can help shape it up. Clear some of these little fish out, and who knows what will happen?"

The boys exchanged glances and were silent for a few seconds, but eventually they went along.

"OK." Jason spoke for them all. "Let's haul a bunch of these babies in. It's not like they're hard to catch or anything."

We found several five-gallon buckets near the sign and set up an efficient little catch-and-release brigade. Two of us would catch one four-inch bluegill after another and flip them into buckets one-third full of water. The other two would lug buckets up the eastern hill and unload them into some tiling Engelsman had put into place. Gravity then took those voracious little fish sluicing down into a nearby creek.

About three hundred bluegills later, I felt we had taken a really significant step. Plus it was starting to feel like work.

"There," I claimed, "you were present right from the beginning. Maybe we should try one more cast before we go, out deep along that drop-off, just to see if there's enough room now for any bigger fish from below to get at our bait."

So Joel took his pole and put his bait right on the line where the light water met the dark. As a dozen or more little bluegills instantly slashed around the bobber, I sucked air harshly between clenched front teeth.

Jon was nearest me and looked up sharply when he heard.

"Aw, get real, Dad. Anybody can see this pond's going to need more than an afternoon's work. It's a good thing the three of us memorized the directions, huh?" ☙

Heart Trouble

R ight across from our house on the street where I grew up
lived a Hulk-like man all the kids secretly called Sidley (his
real name was Sidney). I never got to know him very well, but I
will never forget two things about him.

One was his voice. I have no idea how I had built up all the
stereotypes that I had as a boy, but whenever I heard Sidley talking, I had to bite the back edges of my tongue to keep from
laughing. Here was this huge man with an extremely high-
pitched voice; he had something close to a boy soprano's voice
in a lumberjack's body.

The other thing was that every spring he and his brothers
and dad drove up around Lake Superior to Wawa and then flew
to an outpost cabin to fish for northern pike. When he got back
from one of these trips and spotted my dad shooting baskets
with my two younger brothers and me, he would walk across
the street to tell his tales.

"You wouldn't believe it," he'd say. "We'd row out from
shore only about a hundred yards, cast some floating Rapalas toward the reeds, and suddenly it was thunder and lightning.
We'd land a lot of those pike, but some of the real monsters
would tear off parts of our lures, swirl around on the surface,

and then swim away in scorn." Occasionally he'd bring along a peck basket, lift out damaged lures one by one, and give us the details of what he called each one's "mangle-ation."

His stories both fascinated and frightened me. I would love, I thought, fighting a giant pike, even for a few seconds, but I would also be afraid, I was pretty sure, of handling such a fish if we got it near or in the boat. Some of those pike, Sidley said, could bite off a grown man's hand.

My dad, though, seemed utterly fascinated by Sidley's tales. He would listen intently, often shift his gaze out to the north, and ask all kinds of questions — questions about how long it took to fly to their cabin, how high above the trees the plane flew, how often a plane flew over to check on them, and what they would do if someone did something stupid or clumsy, like chopping off a toe or two when splitting firewood. "Having us all together on a trip like that would be incredible, just incredible, wouldn't it, boys?" he would say.

But he never took my two younger brothers and me to Canada to fish. He usually took us camping on one of the ovals at Holland State Park. There my brothers and I would crawl out of sleeping bags early to claim a prime spot on the north breakwater, where we would often catch enough perch for lunch for our whole family. The perch were fun to catch, manically twisting bodies of yellow and orange. When we came back to our campsite and showed them off, occasionally Dad would say something like, "They're not huge, but they taste great. Since you're obviously getting to be such good fishermen, maybe someday before you're all out of the house we'll have to book one of those fly-ins for pike."

But he must not have figured how fast we would grow up

and move out of the house, since while we were at home we never drove north of the Soo and took off in a floatplane.

So during my first year of teaching, near Chicago, I decided that there could be no better surprise gift for my dad and brothers than if I were to go ahead and arrange for a fly-in trip for all of us. I watched the papers closely, and when the All-Canada show came to Chicago, I spent quite a bit of sweaty time edging past people crowded around the various booths until I found an outfitter who for a reasonable price would fly us to a wilderness lake an hour or so north of Hawk Junction.

I waited until I stopped back home during my spring break to surprise my brothers and my dad with the news. When they heard, my brothers went wild, prancing around the house calling each other names like Pierre and Jean-Jacques because they suddenly imagined themselves as voyageurs. With all this commotion, it took me a while to notice that Dad hadn't said a thing and was looking wistfully out into the backyard.

"Dad," I asked, "what's up? Is that week a bad time?"

"No, not especially; it's great all the planning you've done, and you guys should go, you really should — I'm sure the fishing will be great — but I can't see how I could ever go."

My brothers stopped their cavorting. And I had to swallow before I spoke: "You can't? Why not? We've been talking about this kind of trip since all of us boys were too small to row a boat straight."

"Yeah, I know, but I can't, I just can't. These days there's no way I can see myself spending time so far away from a hospital. I don't want to start having chest pains and then have to worry about getting a plane to come pick me up. And did you ever think what it would be like to haul a corpse out of the wilds? You guys just go without me."

But without our dad, what had looked like the adventure of a lifetime seemed more scary than exciting. We boys decided to plan a fishing trip closer to home. And Dad insisted that he pay me the percentage of the down payment I would forfeit.

Not quite a year before I had done this planning in vain, Dad had had a heart attack. At the time, he was only forty-seven years old.

For weeks before his attack, I had heard him complaining to my mom that it seemed impossible to meet the deadlines at work, and he had started to go in to the tool and die shop on Saturdays, when no one else was ever around, to try to catch up. But on that one Saturday in September, he woke up, he said, with a little tightness in his left arm. Studying a blueprint at work, he was startled when drops of sweat fell from his forehead and started to wash out markings on the paper. Then suddenly he was nauseated, so suddenly that he had to drop to his knees and use the closest receptacle, his own wastepaper basket, to vomit into. Soon he started to feel, he said, "as if an elephant was standing on my chest." This pressure became so intense that he barely managed to crawl over to his desk and call my mom for help. Later, he couldn't remember a word that either of them had said.

When I got home from work later that day and was stuffing gear in a gym bag to head out to the beach for some volleyball, Barb, my little sister, came downstairs and announced that Dad was in the hospital after having "a little heart attack."

My very first reaction, I remember, was pure annoyance: Why now, right on the day that a dozen friends and I had been looking forward to all week? My next reaction was disbelief: He's only forty-seven years old; guys forty-seven years old don't have heart attacks; guys forty-seven years old still play basketball with their kids. And what did she mean by "a little heart attack," anyway?

If it was so little, why, when I saw him in the intensive-care unit, did he have more tubes than I could keep track of dangling from various machines and snaking into his nose, his arm, and under the sheets to places I couldn't see? As I tried both to trace these tubes and figure out what all the flashing numbers and wavy lines on the machines meant, I started to see thin little stars, pinpricks of light flashing before my eyes. Then the arms grew longer and thicker until the stars melded into one another and my field of vision was completely whited out. Somehow, it also seemed that I could hear the very valves in my heart working.

"I need to sit down, I think."

And then my dad, as from afar: "Get that kid out of here. He's going to fall and smash about a million dollars worth of equipment."

A nurse helped me to a chair, coached me into steadier breathing, and after a few minutes the whiteness and the pounding went away.

After about a week and a half in the hospital, Dad came home to finish recuperating. His lifestyle was changing in front of our eyes. He wasn't supposed to have much salt in his diet, so if we kids wanted salt on potatoes or beans we had to add it ourselves. Lots of things that he used to eat he now avoided —

he'd carefully cut the fat ("suet," my Grandma Reka called it) off beef roasts and didn't dare eat bratwurst or real ice cream. When we passed cheese and crackers around while watching Tiger baseball, he'd take only the crackers.

The doctors told him he'd better start a program of walking. He began with little circuits in our house — kitchen to living room to front hallway, repeat, repeat, repeat. Then he started going up and down our block a couple of times. After a while, he'd walk to Mel's barbershop, a half-mile away, and back.

"Yup, the doctors tell me there's some damage to the heart, but if I exercise more and watch what I eat, I should get a few more beats out of the old ticker. That heart attack might even have been a blessing in disguise, a little wake-up call." Some of his friends had had heart attacks in the recent past, too, but by the time somebody had reached them they were gone.

I knew Dad was trying to reassure us with his frequently repeated line about a "blessing in disguise," but I was always uneasy with this talk because he never succeeded in hiding from me several signs that he was worried about his heart. I saw that he would have to pause and take measured breaths when he and my mom carried groceries in from the car. I noticed that he would drop a hand to his wrist and furtively check his pulse while someone else in a group was talking. Somehow I could almost sense when he was getting ready to fish a plastic pillbox out of his pocket and slide a couple of tiny white pills into the corner of his mouth, usually while pretending to clear his throat. And yet much of the time I found ways not to dwell on these signs.

But when he came right out and told my brothers and me that he didn't dare go fishing in Canada, many of the fears that I had been trying to dismiss hit me with clarity and force. And as I drove back to Chicago after that day of scary revelation, I realized that in the future I would never hear the phone ringing in the same way again.

I also realized that every one of my future prayers, no matter how short and context dependent, would include a petition about my dad's heart. I could hear myself in advance: "Lord, protect me as I drive through this blizzard, and keep my dad from any more heart trouble." Or in another setting: "Lord, make this traffic jam clear up before I run out of gas here in the middle lane of the freeway, and keep my dad's heartbeat strong and regular."

Toward the end of my trip back to Chicago, I also debated whether it was necessary in this world for fear to be handed down with so little loss from one generation to another. Since I was fighting for hope, I resolved that if I were ever to have children myself, I would do everything I could to make sure they would never have to worry about my health. Since I assumed they would like to fish, I also made a pledge to myself to take them fishing in Canada.

By the time I met Wanda, I was running five or six times a week. By the time we had our first son, I was competing in half-marathons. By the time our third son was born, I had taught myself how to cross-country ski and could quite easily ski fifteen to twenty miles.

But as I moved into my forties, I started to feel pinpricks of apprehension about my annual physical exams, because each time the doctor found something new not quite right with me. First it was my blood pressure. The numbers were not terrible, the doctor told me, but they were moderately high, matters of modest concern, certainly high enough for me to see how my body would react to some blood-pressure medication. No sense inviting a stroke. "You teach linguistics, right? You think you'd like losing your own language?" he asked.

Then it was my cholesterol. Even with all the exercise I was doing, I couldn't get my good cholesterol high enough and my bad cholesterol low enough. "One of these new statin drugs should help you," my doctor said.

"I think that's the stuff my dad takes now," I said. "He's always told me I should have picked parents with better genes. All right, I'll take those pills if I have to, and my wife can know, but I'm going to hide them from the kids."

And so my three sons saw me running and skiing and leaving to travel to various races around Michigan. As far as I could tell, I had given them no reason whatsoever to be concerned about my health.

When they careened into adolescence but were clearly more skillful fishermen than I ever had been at their age, I remembered the pledge I had made to myself and visited an All-Canada show for the second time in my life. With the exchange rate so favorable for someone willing to spend American currency, I decided to try something even more extravagant than I had proposed to my dad and brothers. My boys and I would drive to a lodge on an enormous lake bordering a provincial park, and each day a guide would fly us out to a different location to fish. We could fish for brook trout one day, walleye the next, lake trout the next, and pike the day after that. When I told the boys about our trip, their reaction was uncannily like my younger brothers' had been several years before. Only the names they gave themselves were different.

So we made lists and packed equipment and bought lures that were as big as most of the fish we were used to catching. All the while, I worried about what it would be like to fish with all three of them together for so long. I couldn't forget how they had once tossed fishing rods aside as they pursued jumping frogs. And as we drove to the lodge, they clearly showed that they hadn't outgrown their boyish ways, especially when it came to not bothering me, the driver, on the long trip north.

When we were only a little more than an hour away from home, I started to hear that question every parent on a trip hates: "Dude, dad, are we, like, there yet?" And they never left the radio tuned to one station long enough to hear even a single song from start to finish. There I was, belted to my seat and assaulted by six seconds' worth of one kind of music after another — classic rock, seek, country and western, seek, rap, seek, hip hop, seek, gospel, seek. Worse, it wasn't long before teasing began and tempers flared. I would hear the bumps and grunts of serious wrestling in a confined space, and I had to lean backwards over the seat to try to break their fights up. Fortunately, I went onto the shoulder only a couple of times and never lost control of the car.

"It'll have to get better when we reach the lodge," I thought to myself. And it did. During a late-night snack after we had unpacked, Frankie, our guide, showed us a huge map on the knotty-pine wall; stuck in this map were several colored thumbtacks. All of our attention was drawn to the large black pin in a bay of a lake that looked like an upside-down oak leaf.

"That's the pin for Kaiser Richard," Frankie explained, "the biggest and meanest northern pike any of us guides knows about. We'll save him for your last day, when you might be ready to mess with him."

Our first day's destination was marked by a red pin. We would put waders on before we boarded the floatplane, fly for half an hour and land on a broad section of the English River, tie the plane up to the bank, and then walk upstream to fish several streams that fed the English. "Brook trout," Frankie said, "big brook trout. Not those slivers you catch down in the States, but fat and sassy cold-water trout. The prettiest glory of a fish in the universe, eh?"

Somehow I managed to get a little sleep that night, and in the morning I made sure that the boys and I ate several slices of toast so that our stomachs wouldn't be bouncing around as gusts of wind caught the plane. The flight went amazingly quickly, mainly because we were able to spot moose every so often standing on the edges of bogs. And the landing on the river was exciting — dozens of hard skips, a long deep swooshing, and finally the gentle backward rock as we settled on the surface. After he nosed the plane into the bank, Frankie told us to wait in the plane until he had tied us up to some clumps of tag alders. When he gave the signal, I stepped out of the plane and started to work my way along the right pontoon to the shore. After a few steps, I figured I could hop from the pontoon into what looked like a couple of feet of water near the shore. But we were parked over a steep drop off, and the water was clearer than any water I had ever seen outside of a bottle. I stepped into water over my waders, and I sucked breath as the chill went to my groin.

"Whoa, cowboy, you can't walk there!" Frankie shouted. "Water that cold can give the strongest guy a heart attack!"

I was so shocked and embarrassed that all I could do was sputter and try to get my breath back as I sloshed onto the bank. But there was something in Frankie's tone that Jason, our twelve-year-old, apparently didn't like, and from the door of the plane he shot back, pretty heavy on the sass: "A heart attack? Our dad? No way! He's only forty-seven years old." ◐

For the Morrow

For the last thirty minutes of our trip that Friday night, I had to drive through darkness more stifling than anything I had ever experienced outside of a cave. It was the darkness of sparsely populated northern Michigan under a night-time sky that would have left voyageurs arguing about north. It was the darkness of roads tunneling beneath canopies of trees in and near the Manistee National Forest. It was darkness with a will, pressing itself in against the beams of our headlights as they probed narrowly ahead, closing behind us implacably as we passed.

"Please, guys, please," I called over my shoulder to Jon, Joel, and Jason, who were sick of riding and were starting to break into spats of taunting and wrestling in the back of the van. "You've got to help watch out for deer. Call out if you see any yellow glints at all. We don't want any antlers or hooves to come blasting through the windshield. And any time now we should start seeing signs for the lodge. Make sure I don't miss any. I don't want to get lost out here."

We had hoped to get an earlier start north out of Grand Rapids, right after Joel's soccer game. But the game had gone through two overtimes and had still ended in a tie. That made us about an hour later than expected. And it was late fall, about a week after we had set our clocks back, closing in on the darkest time of the year.

I could understand why the boys were impatient to get to the lodge. The brochure had featured pictures of an enormous structure in a meadow sloping down to a grassy bank of the Pere Marquette River. The building was made out of huge pine logs stained a light gold. It included enough bedrooms and bathrooms for all five families on the Vande Kopple side of the clan, a spacious kitchen and dining area, a comfortable sitting room with oversized sofas and a fieldstone fireplace, a recreation room, and a hot tub.

"Go to Ludington, then east on 10 to the second little burg past Scottville — you can find that, right? — then south from the center of the village until you cross a one-lane bridge over the PM," my dad had said, "then back to the east for a few miles and finally just a stone's throw or so more north."

I was heading south looking for the bridge. Finally it came up out of the dark, and Joel yelled out, "There, right on that peeling birch, a little yellow sign: 'Barothy Lodge, next left.' Do I have the night vision or what?"

Suddenly all three boys were hushed and peering ahead, competing to be the first to spot the entrance road. I could hear them breathing huskily at my back.

"Do you think all the cousins will be there already?" Jon asked.

"Probably," Wanda said. "Don't you think so, Bill?"

"Yeah, I'm almost sure they will be. All the others will be waiting for us. And they're probably holding supper until we show up. This is going to be a weekend you'll remember even after you have your own kids — we'll canoe, fish, hike, soak in the hot tub and then run around outside as if brown bats were after us, check out all the expensive toys in the recreation room, and have about as much fun as Dutch people can stand. Just help me look for the entrance road, OK? We should be just about there."

And we were. I drove east for a few more minutes, spotted the entrance road first on my own, followed that narrow roadway along the crests of a few gentle hills and then through young pines until light from the lodge guided us around the last several curves to the parking area. In an enormous picture window, backlit by the intimate glow of several candles and a few lamps with bases that looked like antique lanterns, stood Grandpa and Grandma, each with an arm around the other. It was the eve of their fiftieth wedding anniversary.

"Make sure you congratulate Grandpa and Grandma," I told the boys as I edged the van up to the boulders around the parking area.

"Not to worry, Dad," Jon said. "I wrote a limerick for them at school."

"A limerick? You're sure that's the most appropriate kind of poem for a wedding anniversary?"

"Nope, but my teacher said it's got some pretty interesting stuff in it."

"OK. Well, then, why don't we all go in together, ask Grandpa and Grandma to sit down in some place of honor, and then you can read them your masterpiece?"

But just then their cousin Tim threw open the double doors to the lodge and yelled, "Jon, Joel, Jason — get in here! You can't believe this!" The boys almost took the sliding door of the van off its supports as they burst out and then sprinted for the lodge. As they reached the double doors, however, their Aunt Judy appeared next to Tim and gathered them all up.

"Whoa, whoa, whoa, whoa. I'm in charge of the meal tonight, and I've been keeping it warm while we waited for you tardy souls, so we're all going to sit down together and eat first."

"Aw, Mom, can't I show them the room with the hot tub in the floor, just for a second?" Tim begged.

"Not right now. Eat first, explore later."

Imagine members of three generations of an extended family — Grandpa and Grandma, their four children and their spouses, and eight grandchildren — eating a meal together and somehow avoiding all the usual ways to vex and irritate one another, within and across generations.

In other words, imagine no one referring once again to perfectly useless gifts he or she had received during otherwise long-forgotten Christmas or birthday celebrations. Imagine neither grandparent hinting to any members of the second generation that they had not done nearly as well as another member of that generation in cultivating proper table manners in their children. Imagine no members of the second generation boasting about what they regarded as unmatchable achievements of their own children. Or, finally, imagine no members of the third generation pestering their parents to step in and discipline one or more of their cousins.

All of us, in fact, acted as if we might never again get the chance to share such a meal. And Judy's lasagna was wonderful.

After dinner, their five cousins — already wise in the ways of the lodge — led our sons into a whirlwind exploration of all that the place offered for entertainment. All eight rushed to the sitting room and each tossed a few darts, most of them hitting the board. Then they whirled and ran over to the pool table, where they spent more time arguing about cues and teams than actually playing. From there they skated in their socks down the wooden floor of the main hallway to their rooms, pulled on bathing suits, and then kicked up some froth in the hot tub for three or four minutes. After hopping out and drying off, they hauled all the board games out of a big closet and spread them on the floor of the sitting room, the younger ones scattering dice and chips and colored tokens and play money all over the floor.

"Just about time for grandchildren to go to bed, isn't it?" Grandma called out over the uproar.

"Aw, man, can't the kids just stay up while all the old people go to bed?" Jason whined.

"No way. We've all got to rest to get some strength for to-morrow. It'll be a big day," I jumped in before Grandma had a chance to react to Jason's reference or tone.

"Right," added Grandpa. "Plus as soon as it's light tomor-row, you'll get to check out the river. There might be only one other river in the whole Lower Peninsula prettier than the Pere Marquette. And everyone says the PM holds a bazillion fish."

Since our three sons were almost compulsive about fishing — they had reminded one another repeatedly in the prior week to pack their fishing gear and waders — and since some of their cousins were close to sharing their compulsion while the others at least tolerated it, Grandpa's words worked on the grandchil-dren as all the adults hoped they would. The kids didn't hurry off to bed, but they shuffled off in the general direction of the appropriate bedrooms, and soon we parents were able to nudge them along so they settled down for the night. Since it was quite late, we didn't wait long to follow them.

The next day surprised us with its balminess. The temperature was mild enough for us to go outside in sandals, shorts, and t-shirts. It felt as if there were no breeze whatsoever, and the usually gossipy poplar leaves confirmed this feeling with their quiet. The sky was clear except for several strands of cirrus; it seemed as if someone had laid down a swath of fresh cotton far in the west, behind the tree line, and then had worked delicately to tease wisps of it off to the east.

Travel bureaus would probably have advertised the day as a perfect example of fall in Michigan had so many trees not already lost most of their color. The oaks in northern Michigan had gone down from scarlet to rust. The maples had gone down from searing orange to shades of wet clay. Only the willows near the river, the big-hair trees, showed some streaks of bright color, a little green amid slightly translucent brown.

Since the sun was quite bright, however, we adults of the second generation had trouble getting Grandpa and Grandma to leave the lodge. Several days earlier, they had had an appointment with their dermatologist, and each had had some precancerous spots on their skin frozen. Most of Grandma's trouble spots were on her hands and forearms, and the treatment had left her with several scab-like spots that we guessed were once reddish but were now changing to bluish black. Grandpa's main trouble spot had been on his right ear, on which he showed a bulging yellow blister on the topmost inside ridge.

"We know it's nice outside, but that doesn't matter. We can't go out in the sun," Grandma countered our coaxing.

"That's the truth — strict instructions from the doc," Grandpa added. "It's probably because of too much sun when we were young that we've got to be checked for these spots all the time now anyway."

"All you've got to do is cover up," I urged. "I'm sure we've got at least two hats with wide brims around here. And I've got some gloves in the van. They might smell like motor oil a little, but no one would say they stink. You've got to come outside. You've got to see what the kids are doing in the river."

"Are they OK?" Grandma worried. "They're not going to fall in and drown, are they?"

"No, no, not at all. Grandpa was right — the river's full of fish, and it took the kids about three minutes after breakfast to discover them. Now they're out there having a blast trying to catch them. The ones who didn't pack fishing tackle are the designated netters for the fish that the others hook."

Just then Matt, the youngest of all the grandchildren, backed his way up to the deck, dragging an enormous fish, probably about twenty pounds, its gill covers working desperately as Matt turned and struggled to lift the fish up by the tail for display.

"My, my, my, my, my! Where on God's good earth did you find that fish, Matt?" Grandma almost gasped.

"Joel caught it, just up the river, behind those pricker bushes. He hooked and fought it, yelling the whole time that the fish was a fool to mess with him, while I sneaked down the river below the fish and finally netted it. They might have other ones on right now, but I got so excited I have to go pee. Bad."

Seeing the fish and hearing about the drama of its capture were enough, finally, to get Grandpa and Grandma to cover up and walk out with all the rest of us adults to the river. From the bank we could see that all the grandchildren except for Matt, some in waders, some in shorts and tennis shoes, and one with bare feet, were scattered up and down a hundred-yard stretch of the river and were almost manic with activity. Some, including Jon, Joel, and Jason, were casting spinners or artificial egg sacks to especially large fish finning on scooped-out beds of gravel or to sleeker ones swooping around behind them. The other kids were hopping around from river to rocks and from rocks to gravel spits to try to find the best spot from which to net the fish their cousins might hook. But all of them, without exception, clearly were thinking of nothing but what was swimming in the river.

"Those fish are huge," Grandma whispered. "What kind are they, anyway?"

"King salmon. Chinooks," I whispered back. "The big ones, the fat ones, are females, and they've either dropped eggs in those shallow depressions or will be dropping them pretty soon. Watch for the shimmy. Those skinnier ones behind the females are the males, and they're competing for the chance to fertilize the eggs."

"But will they bite?" Grandpa cut in. "I always heard that once king salmon leave the big lake for their spawning runs in rivers they stop being interested in food. How in the world did Joel get that one — do you think he snagged it?"

"Well, maybe, but probably not," I came back. "The boys and I take a couple of trips each fall to fish for salmon below Tippy Dam, and we've learned that spawning kings won't chase a bait — they're not really aggressive — but if you manage to float bait right down in front of their snoots, they'll sometimes take it in. It must be a kind of reflex."

"But look at them," Grandpa went on. "They all have whitish rims on their tails. And some streaks of white or dull orange on their fins. Those are the colors of rot. And over there, in the slack water behind that boulder, are a couple of fish that look as if they can hardly move anymore. If they got out in the current, they'd be washed away. These fish are going to spawn and then die and stink up the shoreline. Probably they're so far gone now that they're completely inedible. Aren't there any fish in the river that aren't about to croak?"

"Probably," I said. "Steelhead usually run up these rivers in the fall too, but they're not here to spawn. They come up to feed on the salmon eggs that get washed out of the beds and go floating downstream. If there are steelhead in the river, they won't be way up on those gravel beds — they'll be lying in wait behind the salmon, probably in the holes below the spawning territory."

Grandpa went on: "Well, why don't the kids try for steelhead? Go after something that's not half dead? Try to catch something that's not falling apart?"

"They could, but they're probably better off settling for these old kings. For one thing, most of the spawned-out fish won't fight as hard as fall-run steelhead would. The salmon will still fight plenty hard, mainly because they're so heavy, but hooking into a fall-run steelhead is like hooking a prodded bull. Then we really would have to worry about kids getting pulled into holes over their heads. But more than that, steelhead are about as tough as anything in freshwater to catch. You've got to float bait downstream into their faces at exactly the speed of the current below the surface. You've got to use the lightest line you can get away with — they see and shy away from visible line.

And it's hard to feel the bites. It's a really subtle take; if you're not used to it, you won't know that a steelhead is on, and if you don't set the hook right away, the fish will be gone. Roughneck kids and steelhead aren't going to go together. We should just let them have their fun with the salmon. In all the rest of their lives, they'll probably never have another day with so many fish and no other anglers around to try to take over their spots."

"Well, maybe. But it seems weird — chasing all this near-death," said Grandpa.

For a while we adults strolled up and down the riverbank, watching the kids moving below looking for salmon, casting to salmon, and then desperately trying to control hooked fish and get them in a net. But after about twenty minutes, Grandma said that now that she and Grandpa were outside, they should try to find the large enclosure on the grounds that was advertised as holding an exotic species of deer. The other adults decided to go with them, talking about taking a short loop of a hike through the woods after they had checked out the deer.

I didn't care how exotic the deer were — I had seen plenty of different kinds of deer in my life. For me, all the wild action in the river was much more compelling; I wanted to get into the water with the kids. So I hustled back to the van, found my waders stashed in the back, and joined the young anglers and netters. I would stand on a boulder and help them spot the salmon, looking mainly for groups of fish lined up next to one another in prime bedding spots. When a nephew or niece with a net chased a hooked fish off downstream and got into water that was growing scary in its depth, he or she would turn and yell back to me, "Uncle Bill — you gotta go out after this one. I'm almost up to my neck!"

So I would accept the net from trembling hands and chase the fish to where the dull brown of submerged rocks disappeared into the black of deep holes and reach out with the net as far as I could, straining to lean forward maybe just an inch more, sometimes taking water over the top of my waders, gasping as the cold seeped first to my stomach and then to my groin.

"Yowie!" I would yell.

"What's wrong?" the niece or nephew would call over. "Are you scared to go out in the deep parts?"

"No. Just water in the wrong places. You'd think water this cold would be frozen."

But I was willing to pay the price, since I managed to net many of the kings that the kids had hooked, and each capture led to a communal celebration, complete with crazy dances, evolving chants, and energetic tumbling runs that avoided most of the goose droppings in the meadow.

Around one o'clock, someone rang the large bell outside the lodge, signaling, I assumed, that one of our cafeteria-style lunches was available. But none of the kids wanted to leave the river, and I thought that the oatmeal I had had for breakfast would hold me for a while, so I decided to stay busy with them.

Almost three hours later, though, I was hungry enough to be on the edge of cramps. And my lower back had started to tighten up.

"I've got to sit down for a while, and probably I should grab a snack," I thought. So I lumbered in wet waders out of the river and across the meadow to the deck of the lodge, where I peeled the waders off and stretched out my legs, allowing my wool pants and socks to give off the water and sweat that they had soaked up.

Grandma had seen me come up to the deck, and she brought me a large bowl of homemade vegetable-beef soup, hot from the microwave.

"Thanks. This will be great. I'm a lot hungrier than I thought."

"I'm sure. I thought you'd be smart enough to know you shouldn't skip lunch. Neither should the kids. They're still growing. Are they still all right down there? They're not taking any chances, are they?"

When I assured her that they were all fine, she went back to a game of hearts inside and left me alone on the deck. The soup was exquisite. I swallowed the vegetables and chunks of beef and then swished some broth slowly around my teeth.

"Savor it," I thought; "just savor it."

But I noticed that, despite the fact that it was only late afternoon, the rays from the sun had become somewhat burnished and were coming in on a pronounced slant. And then a feeling that I hadn't had in years took me by surprise. I had always hated this feeling when it would first appear. I had always hated it when it grew so powerful that it was the sum of my thought. And once it had left, I had always hated having to fear it would return.

I had had this feeling for the very first time when I was about twelve years old, near the end of one of our family vacations. Each year for the week leading up to Labor Day, my family and maybe twenty-five other families from our church would drive up to Ludington State Park and camp together on one of the Beechwood loops. It was impossible to imagine how those weeks could have been any more idyllic than they were. We would hike, fish, body-surf in Lake Michigan when the waves were up and swim in Hamlin Lake when they weren't, have communal hot-dog roasts, drive to the House of Flavors and challenge one another to eat the four scoops of ice cream in a Pig's Dinner, and sit around stoked campfires, singing all kinds of songs, trying not to ignite marshmallows on flimsy sticks, and listening to adults exaggerate details of stories so wildly that they could have been accused of lying.

The feeling had come on Labor Day, the last day of our vacation and what we all regarded as the last day of summer. Each Labor Day we would get up early and begin packing all our camping gear. Once all the families were packed, we would gather at a picnic area below the dam for a final hot-dog roast. Then we would head to Lake Michigan for a final body-surfing contest, drive down the shoreline into town for a last Pig's Dinner, and finally leave for home.

I had first noticed the feeling in the morning, like the first twinges of an impending headache, as I stood next to a few men from my church in the bathroom brushing my teeth and watching them shave. But it had really intensified as we swam. I had hit a wave just right, ridden it for fifteen or twenty yards, scrambled to get my legs under me and shake the water out of my ears, and then stared out away from shore to a distant series of sandbars where waves were breaking and churning up silty storms.

"It's the last time this summer all my friends and I are going to be together," I had realized. "No more hikes to the lighthouse, no more fishing in the lagoons of Lost Lake, no more hot-dog roasts on the dunes, no more stories around campfires, no more of just about everything good."

And at the time, it had seemed as if I would never again be

able to enjoy an activity without worrying obsessively about its inevitable end. ⌡

As I had stared out to the sandbars, almost panting to try to fight off the black shakes, my dad had come out of a body-surfing run within a yard or two of me, stood up, brushed the hair out of his eyes, focused on me, and noticed I wasn't doing too well.

"What is it? What's wrong?" he had asked.

I had tried to explain, blubbering more than I had in years, and I had feared that he would snicker at me and tell me I was old enough to know better, to be stronger, especially since my little brothers were around.

But he had surprised me: "I know what you mean. I feel that way a lot too — especially up here around Labor Day. It's awful, a black pit with snot on the sides. Don't blame yourself. It's not your fault. It very well could be my fault — I've probably handed this down to you wrapped up in some rotten gene. But you can fight it. You've got to fight it. You know we're going to be back here again next year. How many years now has it been that we've been coming up here this time of year? Since before you can even remember. So can you try to look ahead — and look with hope? Do you remember what my favorite line from a hymn is?"

"Huh? A line from a hymn?"

"Sure. You know — 'strength for today and bright hope for tomorrow.' It carries me through a lot."

"Oh, yeah, I remember that. I can try. I guess I have to try. Thanks. Thanks a lot, Dad." But as we had turned and started to push out to look for the next good wave, I hadn't been able to choke off the voice reminding me that for various reasons some families that once had been with us at Ludington no longer were able to come. And Rich the piano tuner, my dad's best friend, the best body surfer anyone in our church had ever seen, the one who was supposed to be the biggest health nut around, had surprised everyone some months earlier by falling down dead from a heart attack, when he was only in his forties. But as I had promised my dad, I had tried.

Later that day I had been surprised to realize that the feeling had mostly pulled back. But it had returned during subsequent family trips to Ludington, sometimes scaring me a day or two before we even made it to Labor Day.

As I had grown older and started taking vacations with my friends, vacations involving long and strenuous backpacking and canoeing trips, only rarely had the feeling attacked. And after I met Wanda and we started to be busy with our own sons, helping them try to learn everything from hitting a ball off a tee and running to the right base to casting accurately for trout, I had almost succeeded in forgetting that horrid feeling.

So why was it back now, as I stretched out on the deck of a magnificent lodge in the late afternoon of one of the most special family celebrations of my life? It was about enough to make me curse loudly enough for the kids to hear.

I heard the sliding door to the lodge open. My dad came out and pulled up a chair directly across from me. He didn't say a thing, but somehow I knew that he knew I was trying to fight off a demon he was acquainted with. He had probably been watching me from the recreation room.

Finally he said something: "Have your fishing gear in the car?"

"Yeah. I didn't bother to get it out because I was so busy helping to net fish for the kids."

"If I wanted to catch a steelhead, could you rig me up right?"

"Aw, come on. Let's not have any jokes about fishing. This is not toss a bobber and a gob of worms out in the river. We're talking about steelhead. We're talking about ultra finesse, years of practice, thousands of drifts to develop a feel. And you don't really like to fish. Don't you remember all the times the boys and I invited you along on fishing trips and you somehow found other stuff to do? Or if you went along, you hardly ever really fished. How many times have you fished since that time you went with Joel and me to Drummond Island?"

"Big deal if I haven't fished all that much. If I wanted to catch a steelhead, how would I go about it? You going to give me some help here or not?"

"I don't think you're serious."

"I am too — I'm as serious as can be. I'm going to go down there below the kids and catch a steelhead. Bright silver, a rub of pink at the gills, muscles toned in cold water — I've heard about them."

"OK. You can try. But I think all you'll get is a sore arm from casting. Here are my waders. I'll go get my rod."

When I was back, I rigged my rod and line up dropper style — main line to one eye of a three-way swivel, a short piece of line with three small attached sinkers to the second eye, and a four-foot length of leader ending in a small yarn fly to the third eye.

"Here you go," I said. "I've even used fluorocarbon leader — it's practically invisible in the water. If any set-up can fool a steelhead, this one can, so if you don't catch one, don't blame the equipment. Just remember: Look for the deeper runs and pools, especially the pools below spawning beds, cast about forty-five degrees upstream and drift through the pool, try not to let slack line drag in the current, and pay especially close attention just as the fly begins to rise at the end of the drift. Steelhead aren't going to yank the rod out of your hand; it'll be a tap, a little something different from the ticking of your sinkers on the rocks. There you go; you should be all set."

"Aren't you coming along? I thought you'd want to watch something magnificent."

"Nah. I'm going to stay here and try to get these kinks out of my back. It almost went into spasms when I was leaning out trying to net those kings."

What I didn't say is that there are some things I thought a son should never have to watch, things that are too painful, such as when his father makes attempts that will almost surely end not just in failure but in pathetic failure. Besides, now that my dark feeling had found me still vulnerable after all these years, I thought I had better try to figure out once and for all what was happening to me.

"OK. It's your choice. But you'll be sorry not seeing what the old man can do."

"Just don't put any strain on your heart. And don't fall in and get pulled under some sunken log. I don't want to have to rush over and rescue you."

"That's the last thing you'll have to do," he shot back and started off across the meadow, holding the leader up in the waning light, checking, I guessed, whether the line really was invisible.

As he disappeared below the level of the bank, all the questions started to clamor in my head: "Why couldn't it be something that I had actually brought on somehow? Smoke and you'll probably get lung cancer — that made a kind of sense. But this had come out of nowhere for no reason that I could think of. Or why couldn't it be something that I could fight, maybe even control? I could go on a special diet. I could start an intensive exercise program. Really now, was it necessary in the first place for a twelve-year-old kid to be afflicted? And why is it back now, after decades? Was it really not my fault, as my dad had suggested long ago, or had I in fact done something to deserve it? Is it supposed to do me some kind of good, like some personalized thorn in the flesh? How, really, can this be anywhere close to the way things are supposed to be?"

And then, from downriver, a scream: "Dad! Dad! Hurry! It's Grampa! Hurry, hurry, hurry!"

It had to be Jason — only he ever called his grandfather "Grampa."

Adrenaline seemed close to popping the skin off my ears.

"What now?" I choked. "Please not a heart attack on his own anniversary."

I got up, realized that I had no shoes on, yanked off my socks, and tore off across the meadow in bare feet. I ran around a few scrubby bushes and right through the hanging arms of a willow until I reached a spot on the bank where some seepage had eroded a little slide down to the water.

And then, twenty-five yards downstream from me, I saw: Dad on his knees on the edge of a little sandbar slanting out along a pool, Dad cupping his left hand over his mouth, Dad apparently giving no thought to the fact that my rod and reel lay behind him in the sand, Dad with his chest heaving, Dad using his right hand to lift toward Jason and Matt about a fifteen-pound steelhead.

I saw the light from the setting sun as something between gray and purple, with a slight advantage to the purple, but somehow this fish hung in the air as if floating in a spotlight of silver.

Jason and Matt began kicking their way around their grandpa in a wild riverine dance, throwing back their heads and yip, yip, yipping to the sky like wolf pups sensing a meal after days of hunger. They were almost out of control. When they stopped their dance, they stooped over and began to beat the surface of the river with their palms, drumming as if in a frenzy, stopping suddenly and bringing their hands to their foreheads, gurgling with laughter as tiny streams of water flowed down their faces and into their mouths. It was clearly joy that was driving them. But it was impossible, I was sure, for them to know everything their grandpa had just done.

I surf-hopped down the slide and ran with the current without bothering to try to roll up my pants. As I splashed noisily toward the triumphal group, Jason and Matt climbed back onto the bank and ran past me going the other way, rushing to spread the news. Before I could reach Dad, I saw him revive and then release the fish. After he did so, he washed his hands off lightly in the stream.

"What?" I panted as I reached him. "What did you — ? How in the world — ?"

"Bright hope, Bill, bright hope." ◎

Through the Ice

I haven't read all the material that the Iowa Division of Tourism makes available to prospective and actual visitors. Still, I'm quite sure that the state has never spent much money advertising Sandy Hollow City Park, which almost seems to be trying to hide in a shallow depression about three miles east of Sioux Center, drawing the fields of corn and soybeans up tightly around itself.

After all, the park is only a matter of three old water-filled gravel pits whose shorelines have been smoothed down and spruced up, a picnic area with a campfire pit half full of assorted beer-bottle shards, and a forty-unit campground with pines that still need support wires to stand against the winds that use South Dakota to build their relentless momentum.

Sandy Hollow, however, had always been a site of burbling laughter for our thirteen-year-old son Jason. It was there that he spent what he called the "only vacation-like" times of our family's annual summer trips to visit my wife's parents and siblings in northwest Iowa. For Sandy Hollow was where he and the person he called his "Grampa-in-Iowa" went to fish after sneaking away from gatherings that seemed to be developing into full-blown family reunions. Often I sneaked away with them — to fish a little, to read, to watch.

I don't believe Grampa and Jason ever debated what the best way to fool fish was. Largely because of differences in physical capabilities, they simply went about their fishing in markedly different ways.

Grampa had spent decades moving between and behind dairy cows, some of which would kick first and look around later or not at all. Both of his knees were permanently swollen, and his left knee hardly flexed at all anymore. So he would back his pickup as close to the shore of the largest gravel pit as he dared. Then he would use a folded-up aluminum chair for support as he made his halting way onto a sandbar that curved from the shoreline into the water. He would balance his weight on the chair with his left hand, wrench his entire right side around and ahead a foot or so, shift most of his weight to his right leg, and then drag his left foot sideways through the sand until he was ready to reposition the chair and throw his right side ahead once more. When he reached the tip of the bar, he would unfold the chair and fall back into it, gradually listing to one side or the other as the chair settled unevenly into the moist sand.

Jason always brought him his gear, which was simple but effective: a spinning rod and reel, a float that Grampa called a "dobber," a cottage-cheese container full of moist newspaper shreds and worms recently dug from his garden, a small box of hooks, and a stringer for the perch and sunfish that he loved to take home and fry for lunch. Once Grampa was in position, he never moved; he stayed in his chair on the end of that sandbar, leaning to one side or the other, but always grinning with patient expectation.

Jason never used anything but artificial lures — usually he

alternated among a chartreuse plastic frog, a blue-and-cream floating minnow, and a mottled jitterbug. And he never stayed in one spot for more than a minute or two. He would trot to a small spit of gravel, cast, cast, cast in a semicircle out in front of him, dart down the shoreline to a small cluster of rocks, cast, cast, cast again, and thus make his active way around the pond, often almost stumbling as he reached down to pull burrs off his socks as he hurried from one casting spot to the next.

But each time he either caught a fish or saw that Grampa was fighting one, he would hustle back to Grampa's sandbar. Together they would admire the fish from several angles, debate whether it was a keeper or not, brag about who had so far caught the most impressive fish, and make all sorts of emphatic gestures. After each of these small celebrations, Jason would trot off to another spot along the shore.

And thus our son and his Grampa fished, the boy making several more or less extended forays along the shoreline, his Grampa waiting expectantly for him to return.

Indian Hills Nursing and Rehabilitation Home spreads out its several wings high in the hills on the north side of Sioux City. When my family and I got out of our van there last December to visit Grampa a few weeks after his cancer surgery, we could see across thousands of acres of farmland to the east. When we got inside room E-12, we could also see that Grampa had probably barely survived the operation.

It can't really be easy for anyone — not even a pastor after hundreds of visits to sick and despairing parishioners — to spend time walking the hallways and visiting people in nursing homes. For Jason, it was traumatic.

While still in the main corridor, he wondered, "What's up with all this pee smell in here?" Once we got into the room, Jason rushed over to give Grampa a big hug, but Grampa warned him quickly but feebly not to bump the feeding tube that "goes plumb through a hole in my chest and into my stomach." When Jason stepped back somewhat gingerly, he noticed that Grampa's feet were sticking out from beneath the sheet and that he had blue booties on, booties that left his big toes exposed, each with dozens of small puncture wounds.

And then Grampa started to cough. It was a deep, racking cough, a cough that brought up a substance unlike any phlegm or vomit any of us had ever seen — smooth and creamy, not chunky and yellow or green at all. As Wanda rushed to get a Kleenex and soothingly wipe streaks of this cream off her dad's chin and throat and upper chest, Jason crouched down and began taking ragged breaths.

When Grampa settled down enough to try to talk, he began to worry aloud about his physical therapy scheduled for the next day: "That lady is real bossy, almost mean — and strong too. She says she won't rest until she has me taking some steps back and forth in the hallway with a walker. She doesn't know I never did walk too good. And now I don't think I'll ever walk again."

As Grampa finished saying "walk again," Jason got up and ran out of the room.

Wanda and I, and our other two sons, Jon and Joel, spent a little more time with Grampa, working to believe that he wanted to know what had been keeping us busy lately. But it was clear that he was laboring to look interested, so we told him we'd let him rest and would drive down again from Sioux Center the next day.

When we got back to the van, we found Jason sitting on the rear bumper with his head on his knees. Before we could even begin to think of what to say to him, he looked up, wiped his nose on a shirtsleeve, and announced that he was "never coming back to this place."

We were able to stay in Iowa for only five days of our Christmas vacation, and we had planned to visit Grampa every day if the roads were good. But the next day Jason would not be moved: He refused to see Grampa lying in that crib-like bed in the nursing home again.

In times of stress or crisis in our family, our rhetoric gets chaotic. Wanda and I tried strategy after strategy, each for about thirty seconds. We carefully presented an elaborate case, and we threatened punishment. We cajoled, and we bribed. We pleaded, and we displayed ugly little spikes of anger. But we finally realized that if we were going to get Jason to that nursing home again, we would have to carry him thrashing to the driveway and hurl him onto a seat in the back of the van. We decided it wasn't worth it.

We fretted, though, about leaving him by himself at his uncle and aunt's in Sioux Center, where we were staying. So Wanda and I each spent at least fifteen minutes laying out for him all the things he should not even begin to think of doing while we were away, and then we left for Sioux City with Jon and Joel. While we were away, he found something to do that we had not explicitly forbidden, but that was only because it had never occurred to us that he would ever hatch such a plan.

When we got home, we found out from his Uncle Stan what he had done. He apparently spent most of the morning after we left poking around in Stan's shed. There he dug up a small fishing pole, a few jigging spoons in a stowaway box, a large flathead screwdriver, and a framing hammer.

When Stan came home around noon after finishing his morning chores on his acreage, Jason met him at the door and caught him in a barrage of questions: "Can I use all this stuff I found in the shed? Do you still have that old Polaroid camera? Does it work? And is there any way you could drive me out to Sandy Hollow and wait just a bit while I do something important for Grampa?"

Stan, always hospitable, but in this case more than mildly curious, I think, about what his young nephew from Michigan could be up to, said yes to all of Jason's questions, provided, he added, that Jason wasn't planning anything risky.

"No way — you know me, right?" came the reply.

So after the two of them packed some heavy clothes, Stan took Grampa's place next to Jason in a pickup headed out to Sandy Hollow.

Once there, Stan asked no questions; he stayed in the pickup, starting it up every few minutes when he needed to run the heater. Jason collected his gear, walked directly to where he knew the arc of Grampa's sandbar was buried under a few inches of crusty snow, and then scuffed around on the ice until, Stan later reported, he looked to be several feet away from the outside edge of the bar. Then Jason knelt on the ice and started chiseling away at it with the hammer and screwdriver. The ice was at least six inches thick, Stan guessed, and Jason really needed a spud or an auger, but he kept at it, occasionally missing the screwdriver and bruising his hand, frequently sending up ice chips hard into his face. After about ten minutes, he broke through to the water. He hadn't found anything in Stan's shed to skim off the floating ice chips, so he had to take off his left mitten and scoop and slosh the chips out of the hole with his cupped hand. Finally, he shifted back and forth from knee to knee to ease the pressure against his kneecaps before rigging up a spoon on the small pole, lowering the spoon into the hole, and then jigging the spoon in the water of the gravel pit.

Stan told me later that it was at this point that he decided to set a limit — something like thirty minutes or so — on how long he would be willing to sit out at Sandy Hollow in the dead of winter waiting for his nephew to pursue some adolescent dream. But after only five or six minutes, he could see that Jason was fighting a fish, probably a big one. He grabbed the Polaroid, ran down to the edge of the ice, and then shuffled cautiously out to where Jason was carefully sliding onto the ice about a twenty-eight-inch northern pike, one just starting to put on some heavy shoulders.

"Yes! Yes! That's the way we do it!" Jason exulted. "If I hold it up, can you get a picture?"

Jason displayed the fish, Stan took the picture, and then Jason carefully put the fish headfirst down the hole, holding it by the tail to move it gently through the water and get water flowing through its gills. After finally refreshing and releasing the fish, he stood up, brushed the ice and snow off his knees, grinned, and said, "That was awesome. Thanks. We can go back now if you want."

When Jon, Joel, Wanda, and I were still getting out of the car after our trip to Sioux City, Jason met us in the driveway with the pike picture in his hand.

"When you drive down to visit Grampa tomorrow," he said quietly, "show him this."

"What is it?" Wanda wondered. Then with more concern in her voice, she asked, "How on earth did you get this? When did you manage to pull this off? And you want to send just a picture? All by itself? Don't you want to add a little note to explain it to Grampa?"

"No," Jason said as he turned away. "Grampa won't need a note. Just show him." For a moment, Wanda stared at his back, but then she filed the picture away in her purse.

When the four of us walked into room E-12 the next day, it was easy to tell that it was a bad day for Grampa. The physical therapist had been around earlier, he said, to torment him, and he was exhausted. We tried to get him to eat bits of the candied orange slices that we had searched out especially for him, but he complained that lately everything tasted "flau." When we asked him if any doctor had been around earlier in the day to talk about when he might be able to go home, he simply turned on his side away from us, brought the edge of the striped sheet up below his chin, and drew his knees toward his chest.

"Maybe we should just leave for today," Wanda whispered somewhat huskily, emotion starting to choke her from the inside.

"Or maybe we should just show Grampa Jason's Sandy Hollow picture," Jon suggested.

"Yes," Wanda agreed, "how in the world did I forget that?" She found the picture in her purse and then walked around the bed and held it sideways to line it up with Grampa's face.

After he focused on the picture, Grampa was transformed. He reached for the control panel for his bed and raised the top portion until he was sitting up. He took both his upper and lower denture plates out of the glass of water next to his bed and put them hastily into his mouth. He studied the picture for almost a minute. And then he broke into an enormous smile, his eyes glistening, his top plate lying a little crookedly in his mouth and threatening to drop. Finally, he extended his right fist about a foot in front of his right eye and raised the index finger proudly.

"Show Jason this," he said.

"What? What do you mean?" Wanda asked, eagerness and anxiety mixing in her voice. "What should we tell Jason? What do you want him to know?"

"Just show him what I did," Grampa directed; "he won't need any explanation."

The drive from Sioux City to Sioux Center takes about forty-five minutes. For most of that time, Jon, Joel, Wanda, and I debated what Grampa could have meant by the huge grin and display of his index finger.

"He probably meant something like 'We're number one,'" Joel guessed. But that sounded too much like bragging to the rest of us, at least as far as Grampa was concerned.

Jon had seen a movie in which the gesture had figured: "Maybe he means 'there's one true thing.'" But Wanda was pretty sure that Grampa had never watched a movie in his life. He had grown up hearing that television shows and movies were worldly amusements everyone should avoid, and early on he had made those rules his own.

What we all also thought, I'm pretty sure, was that he could have been pointing toward heaven, and while there was comfort in knowing about the assurance that would lead to a gesture with such meaning, we didn't want to think about this possibility much because it meant we would lose Grampa for ourselves. So we all skirted this interpretation in our talk.

When we got back to Sioux Center, we could tell by his smug expression that Jason thought he was in a position of power. It wasn't acceptable behavior for his older brothers to ask him a question that wouldn't embarrass him, so they never mentioned Grampa's gesture. But it was too important a matter to Wanda for her to let it go.

"What do you and Grampa mean when you do this?" she asked as she approximated Grampa's big smile and his finger position.

"Oh, that. Not much. Nothing really." And he tried to look nonchalant, not realizing that his mother was past any mood for stalling or games.

"Please, Jason, please. I really have to know. Please tell me. Right now."

"Oh, all right. That's a signal Grampa and I would give at Sandy Hollow after one or the other of us had caught our first fish of the day. We smiled at each other square in the face and raised that finger."

"But what does it mean?"

"When we did that, we always meant, 'The first of many more to come!'"

This gesture did not come up again in any of our family conversations for about ten weeks — until March, a month cruel enough for us — as we were driving down the long hill past Sandy Hollow on the way to Sioux Center for Grampa's funeral.

It was a dark and stormy day, the clouds scraping their oppressive bottoms on the bare branches in the groves, the fields lying with the brown stubble of last season's harvested crop scattered among the clods. As we passed the drive leading down into Sandy Hollow, Wanda turned to me, brushed my elbow, and whispered: "Do you think he was being ironic?"

"Who?"

"Dad. I mean, do you think he was being ironic when he signaled 'the first of many more to come' to Jason?"

"What's ironic mean?" Jason's voice startled us; we thought all three boys were sleeping in the back of the van.

"Didn't you ever have that word on a vocabulary list in school?" I asked.

"We don't do vocabulary anymore."

"Well, then, when you're ironic," I explained quietly, "you say the opposite of what you really mean. Like if Grampa said 'the first' when he really meant 'no more.'"

Jason thought for only a second or two: "If that's what ironic is, then that's not what we were, especially when we talked about fishing. Grampa and I never had the time to be ironic." ✆

Still Fishing

It was in March, as we drove back to Michigan from Iowa after the funeral for her dad, that Wanda had me make a promise.

I had chosen a lightly traveled secondary road back to the east, mainly because I was not in the mood for trying to hold a space amid roaring traffic on I-80 only a day after staring down into Grandpa's grave and meditating with more than usual seriousness on my "only comfort in life and in death." Plus this road would take us through a part of the state we had never seen before.

Not long after we left, the road started taking us in long sweeps down into and then up out of the broad valley that the Sioux River had washed out as it wound through northwest Iowa. Just as we were on the brink of one more descent, Wanda leaned toward me and whispered, hoping not to wake the boys, who had quickly fallen asleep in the back of the van, "From now on, we're going to have to take as many vacations as we can with whatever extended family we're able to get together."

"Huh? We're driving home from your dad's funeral, and you're thinking about vacations?"

"We'll probably never be able to get your side in Michigan

together with my side in Iowa, but we're going to have to get at least one side together at a time — we've got to give the boys chances to spend really memorable times with the grandparents they have left. The two older boys never really had a good chance to know Dad. When we'd visit before he retired, he'd be milking or cultivating or checking on things at the co-op, and all three boys would be off all day trying to catch minnows in the creek. When we'd visit after Dad retired, he and Jason were able to sneak off to the ponds at Sandy Hollow once in a while, but by then Jon and Joel usually had to stay behind in Michigan and work. Dad's gone now, and those two pretty much missed him. And now that I dare to think about it, I worry that I missed way too much of him myself. When I was little, we never took a vacation as a family — Dad never trusted anyone else to milk his cows. And even if he had found someone he thought he could try to trust, my folks always worried about the cost of going away. After the Depression, they never felt comfortable spending much money, especially on fun stuff. Sure, on the Fourth of July we'd drive to Paullina for the fireworks over the lake, but we never spent even a long weekend camping, hiking, and telling stories around a campfire. When I looked in the casket for the last time, I couldn't fight off the question of how much about him I never knew."

"Is that what this is about? Some remorse about how you and your dad related — or didn't relate? Or maybe even guilt?"

"Maybe a little, but it's more how badly I miss him now that he's gone and I can't do a single thing about it. And no way would I have ever imagined that some of my very own kids would never really get to know my dad."

"Well, we'll probably never learn to like it, but the world has really changed. Right now it's sure not easy getting an extended family together for a vacation. Maybe we just have to let that idea go."

"No, we don't! From now on we've got to try as hard as we can. How do you think it would feel if your mom and dad died and you had to say that the kids really never got to know them? Would that be good for anybody?"

"All right. All right. Why don't I look for places in Indiana, Illinois, and Michigan where we and the rest of my side of the family could get together sometime? And why don't you talk to sisters Judy and Kathy about possible places in Iowa, South Dakota, and Minnesota where we and the rest of your side of the family could get together? I guess we'll have to find a way to come up with the cash for two vacations each summer."

"But I know you're not going to look in all those states; you're just going to look in northern Michigan."

"Maybe, but I know northern Michigan pretty well, and it's a fact that when my family hears the word *vacation*, we think about one direction only — north. So what if I don't search as widely as you and your sisters do? The goal is to find a good place, not to do a wide search just for the sake of searching, right?"

"OK, but promise you'll start looking for a place for this summer already."

"I promise. I'll find a place for my side of the family, just you wait. We'll see how you and your sisters do for your side of the family."

As we spoke, I already had a place in mind. Several years earlier, a little after Labor Day, I had driven to the rapids of the St. Mary's River at the Canadian Soo to try to hit the pink salmon run at its peak. I had been tantalized by stories of 50-fish days and 100-fish days and forearms and wrists that would cramp up after fighting fish that seemed to be pouring ravenously up from Lake Huron.

But my day on the water had been frustrating: The weather for the few days prior to my trip had been warmer than usual, so the pinks hadn't actually turned the crystal-like waters of the rapids dark, as people said they could, and the rapids was so big and varied and beckoning that I never fished one likely looking spot thoroughly.

I would stand on the edge of a pool that looked to be only a few feet deep, but when out of curiosity I started easing myself down the gravel along its side, I discovered that the pool was probably over my head. At the tail end of the pool would be a ledge of bedrock and small boulders, through which a run or two would cut as it led to another pool. This one, too, would spill into another run and then another pool, and these pools and runs extended both upstream and downstream from me farther than I could see. Something had led me to want to check out as many pools as possible, probably the thought that the really fantastic pool would be the next one I discovered. So I had made a cast or two in one pool and then had shuffled gingerly along ledges to the next, ending the day more than a half mile away from where I had crossed to the berm in the morning and seeing many more fish veer away from my shadow than I ever hooked.

So I was a little irritable when I had left the river and had driven back across the bridge to the States. And I wasn't ready just to hop on the freeway and head for home and have to report that I had spent most of the day in one of the more impressive rapids in the world and had almost been skunked.

Instead, I had taken the two-lane road due south from the west end of the Michigan Soo and a half hour later coasted down a long hill toward the main intersection in Cedarville, on the north shore of Lake Huron. Once I was there, it had seemed that all roads led to the marina, and I had decided to park there and walk around on the public docks, seeing channels of emerald water opening into other channels, small islands stringing their way out to points beyond my focus, and here and there shoals that promised cover for fish. And I knew that I had stumbled on water that I had to find time to explore at some point in my life.

So I had driven around the Snows Channel area and found a resort with cabins that weren't obviously sagging unevenly into their foundations, a large central playground area — the light green of grass running up to and moving in broad and unpredictable waves against the deeper green of cedars — and a huge dock from which several kids in baggy swimming suits were lobbing lures out into the boating channel. The resort looked great, so I had collected rental information from the owners; and more than once in the years after that, my boys and I had talked my dad into spending short getaways with us there.

This same resort, I knew, would work for my extended family, especially since it was reasonably close to lots of Upper Peninsula attractions. From there somebody could take a day trip to Tahquamenon Falls to see the root beer boil over the edge, or to Whitefish Point to hunt for agates, or to Sault Sainte Marie to watch ore ships descend into the moist coolness of the locks.

After we got back to Michigan, I surprised Wanda by how quickly I made arrangements for a family get-together in northern Michigan. I found out during which weeks of the coming summer the resort had enough openings for my family. I checked with everyone to find out which of those weeks worked out best, in the process persuading some of my relatives to alter some of their plans for the summer. And finally I sent in a deposit to hold several cottages for the last week in June.

Despite all the negotiating and compromising, not everybody on my side was able to go. My sister, Barb, and her husband had already made plans to drive to the Tetons that summer and said they couldn't get off work for two vacations in one summer. And Bob, my immediately younger brother, was able to get off work for only about half of the week. But my dad and mom were able to go, as well as all of their grandchildren, and getting these generations together had been what Wanda had been most concerned about in the first place.

From the afternoon when all of us stretched out sore muscles as we climbed from our vehicles at the resort, complaining all the while about construction delays and flag persons who seemed to have fallen asleep while standing, we started to learn surprising things about one another.

For one thing, the five boys among the grandchildren — our three as well as their cousins, Tim and Matt — simply could not fathom how their grandpa could consistently beat them at horseshoes and could do so as if he didn't really have to try.

"These are pretty heavy. How do you play this?" they had asked on discovering the horseshoes. And as they looked over the two stakes and associated pits, they carried themselves as if they could whip anyone at the resort. They were young, they were strong in the stringy way that many adolescent boys are, they were arrogant.

"Wanna play?" Grandpa asked as he strolled over. "I'll take on each of you, one at a time. I used to play a little bit when I was younger."

"OK," Joel responded. "Do you want to warm up a little first so you don't hurt yourself? You're playing in the big leagues now, you know."

"Nah, I'm all set; let's get started. Do you want blue or red?"

Within forty-five minutes he had defeated each of his five grandsons and had left them wondering how it was possible to score more than a point or two. Over and over those of us who were sitting nearby watched him and a grandson toss the shoes, walk to the opposite stake, and then bend over and stare down at the shoes in the sand.

"Ah," we could hear him over and over, "that's two for me and zippo for you. I'm not even sure how I do it."

"But isn't this one of mine closer? Don't I get at least one point?"

"No. See: I've got you by about an inch. Two points for me."

The surprise visibly annoyed the boys, and after the last of them had been defeated, the gang of five decided it was time to try out something else, anything else, maybe some beach volleyball. They moved off to the court, wondering aloud as they went about how one person could be "so lucky for so long." But as the week went on, whenever Grandpa was away from the resort, golfing or strolling through town marveling at the prices posted on things called antiques that he remembered using and discarding as a boy, his grandsons again took up the horseshoes and practiced. They whispered among themselves about a challenge coming up at the very end of the week, something they called a "rematch of the ages."

Probably the biggest surprise of the week came at our communal supper on the first day, when Grandma started to describe all the pike fishing she had done with her dad when she was young.

"We were a pair of sly foxes, my dad and I," she stated, no joking at all in her tone. "We'd buy frozen smelt from resort owners. And then we'd anchor off rocky points like those I see up and down the channel here. We'd never use wire leaders. No, no, no. Anybody knows that really big pike can spot a wire leader ten feet away. No, we'd use just six- or eight-pound monofilament tied to a number six hook. Almost always the pike would come in with the line between their teeth, like floss. We hardly ever had a bite-off. And you heard me right; we'd use a little number six hook. Same reason as before — you don't want to let those experienced old pike see your hook. We'd hook a frozen smelt right in the back so that it would suspend as if it were just resting casually. Above the smelt we'd attach a small sinker, and then we'd use a bobber just large enough to suspend the smelt and the sinker. When a pike took the smelt, it wouldn't feel any resistance at all. Watch the bobber move away and under the surface, count to thirty, set the hook hard, and fasten your seatbelts! Sometimes during the fights we had to pull up the anchor and chase the fish. These are pike of the Great Lakes, you know, real twenty-pounders, not those skinny things you boys haul out of the weeds back home."

"Grandma," Jason said, "we had no clue you ever fished."

"Can't live seventy years and tell everything about a person in just thirteen, you know. Those were some fine times, I tell you. And believe it or not, catching those monster pike wasn't even the best part of it. The best part of it was the waiting, the calm. My dad used to call it our 'blessed expectation.' It's a shame you boys never were able to meet him. We'd get those lines out, he'd light up his pipe, and then we'd sit and talk quietly or even play cards. He'd tell me a funny story and then look at me with those big brown eyes, and I'd almost choke since I wanted to laugh so hard but I didn't want to scare any fish away. Oh, what memories are coming back. Now that I've thought about fishing again, it occurs to me that Bill should take me out tomorrow to one of those points down the channel a ways toward the big lake."

"Sure," I said, "if you really want to. How about right after supper? And do any of you boys want to go along?"

The older boys — Jon, Joel, and Tim — said that they wanted to take a boat out by themselves, but Jason and his younger cousin, Matt, wanted to be there when Grandma fought a huge pike.

"I don't care how many boats go out fishing tomorrow," Jason said; "the boat that Grandma and I are in will bring in a trophy! Maybe we should take some kind of flag to tie on the bow."

As it turned out, however, the fishing excursion the next day was not the happy event we all thought it would be.

We did find a rugged point sticking out into the channel, with deep water on both of its sides and pencil reeds along its base near shore. And Grandma had been able to buy some frozen smelt from a bait shop in town. She put two bobbers out, one on either side of where the dull red rocks of the point shaded off into light brown and then disappeared into the depths.

The problem was that Matt, Jason, and I had never sat and fished with bobbers in our lives. We were used to movement, to exploration, to trolling motors and fan casting and checking out the next promising-looking spot we could see. And so were the three older grandsons. So Grandma sat in the bow of our boat, glancing calmly from one of her bobbers to the other, and Matt, Jason, and I lurched around in the open space in the back of the boat, snapping on different lures and casting them everywhere but right around Grandma's bobbers. Every ten minutes or so, the three older boys came drifting by us from the Lake Huron side, throwing out buzz-baits and then reeling them in madly: "Clackclackclackclackclackclackclackclackclackclackclack," those buzz-baits rattled away as they churned across the surface. And of course they had to call over to us: "Got any yet?"

Grandma was patient for about a half hour. Then she had had enough.

"That's it. We can't catch fish this way, all this rocking and rolling and dancing and lurching. And those awful lures the older boys are throwing! It's enough to give a body heartburn! You've got to learn to be quiet. You've got to be still. You've got to be patient. If there was a big fish here when we anchored, it's sure to be long gone now. You think fish can't hear all this racket? They must think we're the dumbest anglers around, having a party with bait in the water! Why don't you take me back to the dock and I'll sit there and fish off the deep-water side of that reef between the swimming area and the main channel?"

In many cases I would have tried to talk her out of going back to the dock so soon, but I knew that her irritation connected to a fundamental view of life, and I didn't think Matt and Jason, poised vulnerably in early adolescence, needed to contend with one of her lectures on the meaning of life while they were on vacation.

When I was younger, I was often expected to sit still and listen respectfully to these lectures. As my brothers and I made our fitful way through high school, and especially as we were about ready to go off to college, she had fretted: "You don't really have to live this way, you know. You boys accept nothing at face value. You demand justification for every last tradition. You challenge the word of every authority. You have to have logical reasons for everything. Always questioning, always pushing, always arguing, never being content. It's scary to me, you and your generation — restless, restless, restless."

It especially worried her when we showed that we couldn't find the tranquil clarity about religious matters that she had. In our teens, we wondered about the age of the earth and about all the dinosaurs that must have lived before anything like an Adam could have walked among fruit trees. Where in Genesis did it talk about dinosaurs? And who were Adam and Eve, really? We read all the stuff about prehistoric skulls being pieced together in gorges and deserts in Africa. Could they have been primitive forms of humankind? And was the Garden of Eden really in Africa? If so, was all that early stuff in the Bible figurative, and if it was, what did it mean for us that it was figurative? When did it stop being figurative?

As we got a little older, we started to wonder about the doctrines we heard so much about in church and home and school. How was it, we would ask, that God could have put something like predestination in place and we could still have free will? That's pretty cheap free will, we would claim. For that matter, if God is truly a loving God, how could he ever single out some people to be damned? And if he did in fact pick out some people to go to Hell, why did our church respond to the Great Commission with so much urgency? Maybe it would be stewardly, we hinted, to put more money into the care of those we were pretty sure were elect and less money into missionary efforts.

Whenever we brought issues like these up, usually at dinner after Sunday-morning sermons, we invariably brought our family to the brink of a crisis.

"They've lost their faith!" my mom would moan. "Or maybe they never had any real faith to start with! How did we fail them so miserably? How can they be my sons? Question, question, question. Argue, argue, argue. It must be the schools. And we thought they were Christian schools. Pay all that money for what? These boys have got to learn to quit picking at everything and accept things. What do they think — get to heaven and spend eternity having big debates with God?"

Maybe I made an ill-advised decision out there in the boat, but I judged that Jason and Matt, simply trying their hardest to catch a big fish in the only way they had ever learned, would probably have their day and maybe their entire week spoiled if Grandma got started about the restless spirits she was certain were already developing in them. So I agreed to take Grandma back to the dock. And when I told them our plans, the three older boys decided to follow us in. "No big ones around here," they complained; "we'll have to try somewhere else. We never felt too sure about this spot."

Once back at the resort, I helped Grandma get set up on the arm of the dock extending into the deepest water. She carried out a folding chair, laid out her bait cooler and tackle neatly behind the chair, and then prepared to toss a bobber into the water between a rust-colored shoal and the big green buoy marking the inside edge of the boating channel.

"Good," she said. "I'll be back in business in a minute. You guys go back and dance around in those boats all you want. I'll stay here and see how long it takes for a big fish to bite. It shouldn't be too long."

So Jason, Matt, and I in one boat and Jon, Joel, and Tim in another headed down the channel in the other direction to a small peninsula, where we leapfrogged each other as we moved around the peninsula, making a few casts and then moving on. Matt thought he might have had a bite, but when he brought his lure in it was dragging a brownish weed covered with tiny snails.

About when the sunset went from pink to purple, Jason looked up and across the channel and said, "Dad, look — there's a big crowd of people out on the end of our dock. I wonder what's going on."

"Yeah, you're right. I wonder too. Let's go back and check. It's just about dark anyway. And the fish haven't exactly been in a cooperative mood."

We hauled up the trolling motor and used the big engine to angle quickly across the boating channel and back toward our dock. The three older boys followed, bouncing noisily in the boat as they cut back and forth across our wake. As we approached the dock, we could see that someone was walking very slowly back and forth in front of the crowd on the end of the dock, a fishing pole throbbing in a desperate arc over the water.

"I'm not sure, but I think it's Grandma," Jason called from

the front of the boat. "It sure looks like Grandma. She's got that floppy pink hat on. And she's fighting a fish. It must be a huge fish! Grandma's fighting a monster! She must not have been fibbing about catching those big pike when she was little. Get in there, Dad, OK? Hurry. But go way around so we don't run over her line."

I did better than go way around; I turned in well short of our dock and pulled up on the little beach on the edge of our resort's property. As the bow scraped up on the sand, Jason and Matt leaped out of the boat and sprinted for the dock. I pulled the boat up higher on the beach and headed for the dock myself, just a few seconds before the older boys beached their boat.

As I was about halfway out to the end, Jason came running back to me. Fighting to catch his breath, he gave me the story:

"She's been fighting that fish for more than twenty minutes already! And the resort owner thinks it's a Great Lakes muskie, maybe even a new state record. It's fighting like a monster fish, they all say. It's not jumping or thrashing around or making a big commotion. It's just cruising along calmly as if it could pull the whole dock in if it wanted to."

By this time, I had come up to Grandma's side.

"A big one, huh?"

"Yeah. When I threw my first bobber out, it no sooner hit the water than it started moving steadily out across the channel. When I set the hook, it felt like I set into a stump. Solid. Just real solid. And then after a few seconds the stump started to move. It's been swimming back and forth here in front of the dock for the last half hour or so. We only got one glimpse of it, but it looks like a muskie, a really heavy muskie. Huge bronze shoulders. I'm taking it easy on it. But I hope it starts to tire out soon. These arms aren't everything they used to be."

"You want any help?"

"Just get a big net out here. This fish thinks it can tire me out, but we'll see who wins out. I didn't fish all those years as a girl to lose a fish like this now. But we'll be needing a really big net."

As I turned to go back to the boat to get a net, Grandma moved calmly off along the edge of the dock, the people making room for her, all of them whispering excitedly, the parents trying to get their kids to keep their voices down, everyone ready to erupt.

The net in our boat, I realized, wasn't big enough for a muskie that might be a state record; I wasn't sure what was big enough for such a fish. But I thought I'd check the little boathouse near the foot of the dock, so I went and poked around in its shadows. In a corner I found a net that looked like it might be big enough. I tried to take my time getting back out to Grandma, but I was too excited to walk. I trotted along, taking care not to hit the occasional raised plank on the dock's surface.

Just as I got back to Grandma's side, the fish made a turn away from the shipping channel and headed directly back toward us. I immediately got down on my stomach on the dock and held the net along the edge of the dock; it looked as if I would have to reach down about three feet to get to the surface of the water.

"Not yet, not yet, not yet — I don't think she's ready," Grandma said as the fish rose to within a foot of the surface and continued to cruise straight at us.

"Holy mackerel!" one of the other guests at the resort called out. "It's headed right toward us."

"I can't believe we let the kids swim in this water," a young mother said. "They should have warning signs posted up and down the channel."

"Hold it steady, hold it, hold it," I called. "I'm pretty sure I can reach it in a second or two."

"I wouldn't go for it yet," Grandma replied. "It looks pretty green yet. It's too early to try — we've got to wait and be sure. I'm not sure I can hold its head up yet."

But then the muskie, even as it continued to move toward the dock, rolled slightly on its side.

"The beast's tired," I hissed back. "It's going over on its side. Bring it in a couple more feet and I can get it."

"I'm not sure I can move it. Oh, OK, it's coming a little. It's like pulling a tree."

"Yeah, yeah, yeah, a little more, that's it, that's it, come to Billy. You're not really as big and bad as you want us to think, are you?"

And then I scooched up as far over the edge as I dared, lowered the net below the surface of the water, and went for the fish's head and upper body.

"Hold my legs down," I yelled. "I'm going over!" Hands clamped down hard on my calves. I got the net under the fish and started to raise it, praying that my lower back would not go out. And for about two blissful seconds I thought we had won the battle. The muskie lay across the net, one side of the net resting under its head, the other side supporting the fish a few inches behind its dorsal fin.

"Fall, baby, fall!" Jason yelled out. "We got you, yes we do!"

But the muskie didn't fold and collapse into the cords of the net. It had enough strength left to flex its body against the sides of the net and then catapult straight up into the air, almost exactly to the level of my face — a huge fish coiled almost into a U with water droplets flying off everywhere. To this day I can remember the exact instant when I saw, just inches before me, the small hook pull delicately out of the corner of its mouth as it fell, banged off one edge of the net, righted itself in the water, flared its gill covers, flicked its tail, and then vanished.

I lay slumped with my head and arms over the edge of the dock. Everything was quiet, quiet and empty. It was all a mockery. How could I face my mom? I had probably just lost the fish of her life. And she had told me to wait.

When I rolled over and sat up, I saw that she was quietly reeling up her slack line. Then she packed up her tackle and made sure the cover to the cooler in which she stored her smelt was on tight. She even took a rag from her jacket and wiped the top of the cooler off, very methodically.

Then she said to me: "Don't worry, Bill. And don't feel bad. I've seen a lot of big fish in my day, I mean a lot of big fish, and I'm not sure that was a record. What's an old lady got to be all hot and bothered about some fishing record, anyway?"

Then to her five grandsons, standing behind her, looking as if they had never witnessed a bigger tragedy, she said: "You know, I've heard these old muskies are pretty territorial. That means that big old fish will probably stay around this part of the channel. If we're patient, we can get her to bite again. We might have to skip some of those day trips we talked about, but you boys have all been up to the locks already, haven't you?"

Then she said to Grandpa, who had been golfing with my youngest brother and had walked up shortly before I lost the fish: "Can you help me carry this tackle back to the cottage? I think I'll leave the chair sitting right here so it will be ready for me in the morning. I'll reintroduce myself to that fish after my morning tea and bran muffin."

"Thank you, Mom," I thought. It would be hard for anyone to give me a more forgiving and gracious opening than that. "She's absolutely right," I said to the boys, even though I still felt hollow. "Tomorrow Grandma can get set up here again on the dock, and we can hop in the boats and work up and down the shoreline in both directions from here. That fish won't be able to hide from us. It had a pretty hungry look in its eyes. Did you see how big its eyes were?"

"We have a plan, then," Grandma said.

"It's a great plan," I said. "I'm going to move our boats around and tie them up; then I'll head in."

The boys walked almost reverently with Grandma up to the cottages while I cleaned the boats out and moved them to their assigned mooring spots. And then I walked up to our cottage, slowly, wondering how the aspens could go from such quivering nervousness in the late afternoon to such breathless calm now. I found that Wanda had made some hot chocolate.

"I heard," she said. "You going to be all right?"

"At first it seemed I wouldn't be all right ever again. But Mom didn't make a big deal of it. In fact, she just talked about getting up early and going after that thing again. The kids are so eager to get out in the boats after that fish that they probably won't sleep. I might have a little trouble myself. I hate to think of what will happen if we don't end up catching that fish this week."

Just then we heard some slight shuffling and scraping on the front porch.

"Boys?" Wanda called.

"Yeah, Mom, we're almost ready to come in. Just a minute."

When they didn't return in four or five minutes, I decided I'd better go out and rustle them up. I stood on the porch but didn't see them. Probably down by the dock, I thought. Halfway there I made out five dark forms of various sizes moving back toward me.

"It's time to come in."

"We know," Jon said. "Just wanted to make sure everything was set for the morning. You tied both of the boats up, right?"

"Yup. I took care of the boats — they aren't going anywhere tonight. Let's all see if we can get some sleep now."

As they walked past me I smiled, thinking of all the energy they were poised to unleash on that fish in the next few days. When I turned to follow them to the cottages, I glanced one last time at the dock. Something was a little off, a little different. What, though? Then I saw what it was: Just on the edge of the whitish light of the security lamp, lined up in a neat row to the right of Grandma's chair, waiting for occupants, were five of the resort's sturdy metal chairs. ⑥

Yesterday, Today, and Tomorrow

In my life as an angler, I have run little risk of thinking too much about the future since circumstances frequently have worked together to haunt me about the past.

Once, for instance, I decided to set aside a day and try for some of the walleyes roaming Hamlin Lake, fish that sportswriters had been raving about in fishing newsletters. I prepared meticulously, even to the point of memorizing most of the details of a hydrographic map of the lake. And then, after working various lures along breaklines on the lake for seven hours and not having a single strike, I complained about my wasted day to another fisherman at the launch site, who replied, "Until this morning the walleyes were hitting practically anything that moved, and then the wind swung around to the east and knocked them a hundred percent off their bite. You shoulda been here yesterday."

Or worse: Another time I decided to steal a couple of days from my regular schedule and try for some of the pink salmon that run in early autumn in dark and enormous subsurface clouds from Lake Huron up the St. Mary's River. Again I prepared meticulously, even bothering to check the line guides on my rods for nicks and scratches. And then, after driving about five hours to the Michigan Soo and spending all of the next day casting as far as I could into the river from various points around the Soo and hooking only two undersized pink salmon, I muttered some complaints before starting home to an attendant at a gas station, who said, "It turned so blasted cold early in August that the pinks started their run three weeks earlier than usual, so now I bet all you can find in the river are some broken-down stragglers that have lost their way. You shoulda been here two weeks ago."

Or maybe worst of all: Late one summer, just before school was about to start up again, my regular fishing buddy, Duzzer, and I managed to carve out an entire week for a trip we had long fantasized aloud about — a trip to northwestern Ontario for northern pike. Again I prepared in detail, even taking the time to make my own wire leaders. And then, after spending nearly fifteen hours in some form of travel and another five days casting around stumps and reeds and rocks in one shallow bay after another and catching only a few small pike that would twirl in the water as we brought them in, I muttered before the flight out to the bush pilot about what an expensive waste of time the trip had been, and he said, "It's been three times as hot this summer than it's been in the past five years for any stretch of eight or more days without four days in a row of rain, so the water in all these bays is much warmer than it usually is. All the twenty-pound-plus pike are probably lying in the muck in holes in forty feet of water sulking. You fellas sure as shinola shoulda come in early June."

Ever since I was nine years old and had the chance to fish on the last afternoon of a family vacation with my dad down along the shoreline from our rented cottage on Hess Lake, when my dad hooked a northern pike and then used a warped oar to dig it and the weeds the fish had buried itself in out of a heavy weedbed, I have wanted to become as fine a fisherman as he seemed to me then.

But since times of missing the good fishing — sometimes just by a matter of hours — have been closer to the rule than the exception for me, I frequently have to fight off leech-like questions about why I have come both to love fishing and yet to fail at it so regularly and miserably.

My questions really come down to two closely related ones: Is there any room in a religious view of creation for pure chance or coincidence? Or does God control everything, from the times you stub your toe to the times when you narrowly avoid a head-on car collision with a semi?

Some of my friends have argued that my experience with my dad and that northern pike — as well as the effects that experience had on me — could very well have been outside God's control. It's not that he isn't powerful or that he can't see as much as some people think, they argue; it's just that he doesn't bother to oversee and get involved with all the small things, such as our little recreational moments.

I have always tried to resist this line of reasoning. In part it's because I have sung "his eye is on the sparrow" often, and I am frequently surprised to find the words of that song echoing around in my head. But mainly it's because I have always seen my experience with my dad at Hess Lake as invested with significant meanings. For instance, I have always seen that experience as the perfectly fitting culmination of so much of my gradually built-up expectation. I have always felt that the fact that the experience happened with my dad made it especially memorable because of our deep personal bond. Finally, the experience had clear marks on my future — it led me to commit myself to becoming a really fine fisherman. Because of all these meanings, I have wanted to believe that God controlled all aspects of the experience. If I could accept that and not doubt, I could see the universe as full of benevolent purpose.

But the more I was able to hold to that belief, the more I was logically led to wonder about the times when I happened to show up late for the good fishing. If God really was behind all that happened that day at Hess Lake, then why thereafter did he put me in the position of having to come home and report that once again I had been skunked? Was God testing me in some way? Setting me up for some lesson? Punishing me?

After one particularly vexing bout with these questions, I resolved that when my own three sons were old enough to fish, I would do everything I could to ensure that they would never have to wonder why they had missed the good fishing.

I decided to be extremely selective about where we would fish: I would avoid the big waters with a reputation for offering hot fishing one day and going dead the next. I decided to take one or more of my sons fishing only when I was certain that the conditions would be favorable: I would study weather maps and charts about phases of the moon so that I could avoid cold fronts, high-pressure areas, and unproductive quarter moons. And I decided to learn as much about fish habits as I could: I would discover what species would bite on what lures at what times in what places under what conditions. In every way that I could imagine, I would control things.

And when my sons were very young, it seemed that often I succeeded. My brother Bob works at The University of Michigan biological field station, about four hours north of Grand Rapids. The main building there is one that even the tree farmers in the area call the Lakeside Lab, a building rising three stories above the shore of Douglas Lake. The most striking feature of this building is its boatwell; its builders cut a channel from the lake through the narrow shoreline into the bottom floor of the lab so that researchers at the station could steer pontoon boats from the lake directly into what is really the basement of the building and moor them there. In planning the boatwell, the architects of the lab were thinking about the advantages of mooring boats out of the elements and in constantly calm water. From the first time that I saw the boatwell, however, I saw it not as a building that could provide safe haven for boats but as the only building I knew about that had been built over a fishing hole.

On the concrete edge of the boatwell people can sit in comfort in lawn chairs. Those people are always protected from wind or rain or snow or sleet. Since there are lights in the lab, people can fish at any time of day or night. And since station administrators want to keep the boatwell from freezing, they keep the lower level of the lab at a constant temperature during the fall and winter. Best of all, I discovered that a school of big rock bass lives in the boatwell and that they become really aggressive biters in the fall. After these discoveries, I knew that the lab was the kind of place where I could safely introduce my sons to fishing.

They weren't very old when the four of us first explored the waters of the boatwell, probably around three, six, and seven. I had bought them some equipment that our local hardware store had had on sale — three-foot fiberglass rods with plastic reels that the boys were especially attracted to, reels with a picture of Mickey Mouse on them. I added to each line a hook with a section of night crawler, a sinker, a small bobber, and we were set. And there we sat, I in my regular-size lawn chair and they in their small ones, not so close to the edge of the boatwell that Wanda would worry about them if she saw them, but not so far away either that they couldn't look over the edge to see if a big rock bass was making their bobber dance.

And dance those bobbers did. From the moment we got bait in the water, we had bobbers shaking and dipping, thirteen-inch rock bass thrashing on the surface as one son or the other yelped, "Help, Dad, help — it's a monster," fish slapping against the sides of the boatwell or flipping off hooks swung high into the air and then flopping on the concrete around our feet, lines being whipped around until they tangled into impossible knots, bare and baited hooks whizzing within millimeters of our ears and noses, and kids slicing night crawlers into chunks with their thumbnails and volleying them around to one another.

It was great.

We naturally lost all track of time and had to fend off some very disapproving looks when we walked in late for a meal at Bob's house, but at the time I could imagine no finer introduction to the joys of fishing than the boatwell had provided.

When the boys got a little older, though, I found a place that came close to rivaling the boatwell. About sixty-five miles north of Grand Rapids is a little town trying to carry the name Paris without any irony, a town that many people heading north out of Grand Rapids used to go through but that now few know anything about since a freeway was cut in around it to the west. If you ever take the time to leave the freeway and take a little detour through Paris, there are probably only a couple of things you'd notice.

One is that on a weathered silo near town is an enormous potato-chip advertisement featuring the silhouette of what appears to be a naked woman. Since I first noticed the figure, ivy vines have acted in the interests of modesty by working to cover the mystery woman with green, but they have known no better than to work rather slowly from her feet up.

The other thing you'd probably notice is that just north of town is a little park built around the pools of what was once a state fish hatchery. There are dozens of pools in the park, and when they were part of the hatchery nearly all of them held fish. Now that the pools are part of a park, however, only the one nearest the park entrance usually has fish in it, but these fish are numerous and glorious, hundreds of three- to four-pound rainbow trout that the town of Paris stocks and rents people equipment to fish for: "Keep everything you catch. We clean and bag. Twenty cents an inch." When I saw the pond, the cruising trout, the sign, and the equipment available for rent, I realized that I had another chance to put a guarantee on a fishing experience for my sons.

The equipment we rented was simple: five-foot fiberglass rods, Zebco reels, small Aberdeen hooks, and tidy plastic containers with our bait — kernels of corn. At first my sons and I thought that catching the rainbows would be as easy as hindsight, but after we worked at it for a while we realized that fishing in such a pool posed a unique challenge: These trout had seen hundreds of hooks baited with a kernel of corn and weren't easily going to fall for them. When a kernel of corn with a hook in it would land on the surface, dozens of them would swerve over to inspect it, but when they got about a foot away from the bait they would all suddenly veer off, somehow never bumping into one another. Each time they did so, they took a little piece out of the guarantee I thought I had.

But can trout fool determined and inventive fishermen forever? Ultimately, some teenagers on the other side of the pool showed us how to outwit these trout. Around the pool stood several containers of fish food. These kids inserted a dime, cupped the released pellets in their palms, tossed a bunch of pellets into a small circle on the surface of the pond, and then cast their hooks baited with corn right into the middle of the fish pellets. The trout would go into a momentary feeding frenzy and lose all ability to distinguish food pellets from corn kernels. Once we observed the tactic, the result was perfectly predictable. Each of my sons tossed a baited hook into the middle of the frenzied fish and reeled one in, giggling uncontrollably throughout the process. They were elated about every aspect of the experience except one: The park attendants only gutted the fish and did not cut off their heads, so on the ride home the dead trout gazed out forlornly at my sons from the freezer bags they had been sealed in.

As my sons grew older, we cautiously expanded the range of our fishing ventures. But as the number of our trips went up, so too did the number of sad surprises. I would hear that the bass were biting on the bayous of Spring Lake, and I would wait for a good day to head out there; then, shortly after one son or the other and I started flipping for bass, the wind would come up and make it practically impossible to keep the boat in a good position to fish from. Or a son and I would head out to Wabasis Lake on a calm and humid night, just before a cold front was supposed to come roaring through, and though the weather would seem perfect while we were on the water, not a single fish would bite.

As such experiences threatened to define our lives on the water, I began to pick up disturbing signs from my sons. Some were not terribly obvious — stifled yawns in the middle of the afternoon. Some were much more obvious: a body hanging limply over the side of the boat and a finger doodling on the surface of the water. Some were impossible to miss: the splash of the landing net while one son or another stabbed for minnows, or the beep of a Gameboy starting up under the cover of a life jacket. Some signs moved into the realm of angler's heresy: requests to "stop in the deep part for just a sec so I can do cannonballs off the side" or pleas to "buy a tube and go tubing before it's time to go back to school."

I was being pressed to admit that, no matter how hard I tried, I could not control our fishing. As my sons grew older still, I gave up pressuring them whenever they seemed reluctant to head out with me. At all costs I wanted to keep them from asking why they had to be the ones showing up a day, two weeks, or a couple of months late for the good fishing.

My sons are young adults now, and it seems very difficult for them to find time to go fishing with me. I still can't forget the call I heard when I was nine, though, and I head out to fish whenever I get a chance.

Since it's hard for me by myself to get my boat on and off the trailer, I generally skip lakes and focus on rivers. So just at the time of my life when it's probably not the smartest thing to be wading on moss-covered rocks, stepping over submerged logs, and edging around holes washed out of sandstone, I fish stretch after stretch of different rivers, always hoping that the next pool will be the one I've been seeking.

I don't worry about hazards in the river or about the danger of having heart trouble in places where ravens almost certainly would become aware of my plight before any humans would. I don't even worry all that much about trying to find out what might be biting when and where and on what fly or lure. It has taken me a painfully long time, but in some ways I have learned simply to try things and hope.

And so it commonly happens that I will be standing below a riffle or a little eddy as the sun starts to throw gold up through the tops of cedars, and I will hear a noise behind me on the bank. My head snaps around, but invariably I need only the briefest of moments, the blink it takes the eyes to focus, to realize that no one is there. It's usually just a dead branch cracking off or a pine cone falling and rolling in the breeze. Yet I know that whenever I hear such a noise in the future, I will not be able to keep my head from turning, a reflex of hope that one day, before I get too old to stand against the currents, the sound will be from one or more of my sons coming down the bank to fish next to me in the stream. ⑥